CREATIVE CAREERS

CREATIVE CAREERS

MAKING A LIVING WITH YOUR IDEAS

B. JEFFREY MADOFF

hachette
BOOKS
New York

Hachette Go, an imprint of Hachette Books
Hachette Book Group
1290 Avenue of the Americas
New York, NY 10104
www.HachetteGo.com
Facebook.com/HachetteGo
Instagram.com/HachetteGo

First Edition: June 2020

Hachette Books is a division of Hachette Book Group, Inc.

The Hachette Go and Hachette Books names and logos are a trademark of the Hachette Book Group, Inc.

The Hachette Speakers Bureau provides a wide range of authors for speaking events. To find out more, go to www.hachettespeakersbureau.com or call (866) 376-6591.

The publisher is not responsible for websites (or their content) that are not owned by the publisher.

Print book interior design by Jeff Williams.

Library of Congress Cataloging-in-Publication Data
Names: Madoff, B. Jeffrey, author.
Title: Creative careers: making a living with your ideas / B. Jeffrey Madoff.
Description: First edition. | New York: Hachette Go, [2020] | Includes index.
Identifiers: LCCN 2019054543 | ISBN 9780738246703 (trade paperback) | ISBN 9780738246710 (ebook)
Subjects: LCSH: Vocational guidance. | Creative ability in business. | Entrepreneurship. | Cultural industries.
Classification: LCC HF5381 .M274 2020 | DDC 650.1—dc23
LC record available at https://lccn.loc.gov/2019054543

ISBNs: 978-0-7382-4670-3 (trade paperback), 978-0-7382-4671-0 (ebook)

Printed in the United States of America

LSC-C

10 9 8 7 6 5 4 3 2 1

CONTENTS

INTRODUCTION

IF YOU COULD HAVE CANDID conversations with people who are open enough to share the stories of their struggles, failures, and successes and learn how they make a living with their creativity, what would you want to ask? I have been fortunate to have that opportunity once a week since 2007 in Creative Careers: Making a Living with Your Ideas, the class I developed for Parsons School of Design, in New York City.

I teach because I love to learn. I have a lot of questions. Questioning is an essential part of learning. It is how we navigate our way to a fuller, more meaningful life. Creativity is how we express who we are. Business is how we support that.

- 💡 How do you define success?
- 💡 How do you assess risk?
- 💡 When do you go all in on your idea?
- 💡 How do you choose what creative battles are worth fighting?
- 💡 How do you attract the people you need when you don't have the money to pay them?
- 💡 Should you raise money, and how do you make a compelling pitch?

This is not a book about how to become the next megawealthy entrepreneur—although it might help you to. Many of us would be fulfilled to pursue the career we want and make enough to live comfortably—which prompts other questions you have to ask yourself: "What do I want? What am I willing to do to get it?"

I graduated from the University of Wisconsin in Madison with a double major in philosophy and psychology. I tried to get a job as a sage, but the wisdom factories weren't hiring, so I got a job in a small clothing boutique. One day a friend of mine called and told me he had saved up some money and asked if I could think of a gig that could earn more than bank interest. I knew what clothes sold and that I could draw, so I said I'd start a clothing company. I knew nothing about design, nothing about getting clothes made. I thought fabric on the bolt was wholesale since it hadn't been made into anything yet. I cut a shirt apart to see how it was constructed.

I had to learn the process of how to turn an idea into an actual piece of wearable clothing, which could be manufactured at a reasonable price, sold to a retailer for a profit, delivered on time, and ultimately sold to a consumer—and get paid. I had to run the business and be creative, designing clothing people would want to buy.

My business grew very quickly. In less than two years I had two factories with more than one hundred employees in Wisconsin, sales reps across the country, and an office in New York. In 1972 I was chosen as one of the top-ten young designers in the United States. There were only eight of us at the time, so it wasn't hard to be in the top ten. This was the very start of the contemporary market in fashion, clothing that appealed to young adults who had a sense of style and didn't want to dress like their parents.

Celebrities were photographed wearing my designs and were featured in national magazines. My clothing was sold in many of the best stores in the country; a fashion company based in Wisconsin was unheard of.

I was twenty-two years old. Unlike today, being a young person with a start-up was unusual. Wanting to express my creativity and make a living doing it was not something that was taught in school. I learned by observing, asking questions, making mistakes, meeting people who were doing what I wanted to do and people who were simply good, knowledgeable people who were willing to share their experiences with me. I also learned who to trust and who not to trust—sometimes too late. There were no courses in school that taught how to make a living with your ideas. I was not prepared for the challenges of being creative and running a business.

I regularly came to New York to buy fabrics and sell to stores. At first I found the city overwhelming. Too many people. Too much noise—but the more time I spent there, the more I wanted to be there. My backer, a banker, lawyer, and very good man, had financed my business because I created jobs for people in Wisconsin. He told me he would not continue to finance my company if I moved to New York. I had a small savings account. Survival money. If I moved, I wouldn't have a job, I didn't know anyone there, and I didn't have a place to live. I was constantly warned about the huge risk I was taking. People asked me if I was afraid of what would happen if I moved. I wasn't. I was afraid of what would happen if I stayed. Money comes and goes. Time only goes. I closed the business and moved to New York.

New York exposed me to all sorts of creative people and had an energy that was seductive and expanded my horizons artistically. Through a contact in the fashion business, I worked with Dennis Hopper, Terry Southern, and William Burroughs, who were trying to put together a film based on Burroughs's book *Junkie*. I realized that film would give me more opportunities to use my storytelling, visual, and collaborative skills. I decided to change careers.

An associate of Burroughs introduced me to some people who were starting a video company to shoot fashion shows, which was a new idea at the time. They were intrigued by my fashion experience. I was intrigued by the medium. I taught myself how to light, shoot, and edit. Within a few months, I had segments on all three major networks.

I decided to start my own company. My first client was the legendary designer Halston. Over the next three decades, I worked with some of the top fashion and beauty brands in the world, including Ralph Lauren, Victoria's Secret, Calvin Klein, Donna Karan, and Estée Lauder, to create video content. I didn't want to just do fashion; I wanted to tell bigger stories, which led to doing brand-positioning pieces for the Harvard School for Public Health, the American Academy of Dramatic Arts, Radio City Music Hall, the Martha Graham Dance Company, and many others outside of fashion.

After a Ralph Lauren show, I was approached by Dean Stadel, a professor at Parsons, who asked me if I would be a guest lecturer in his class. I did and loved doing it. He asked me back every semester for four years.

Dean asked me to develop a course that I could teach on a regular basis. My goal was to create a class that I would want to attend. Creative Careers started in 2007 and has been fully booked every semester. Each week I interview and my students ask questions of high-profile speakers with successful creative careers and listen to them talk about what they do, how they do it, and the obstacles they've had to overcome.

The objective is to break down the walls of perceived differences between businesses—from fashion to visual arts to the start-up world and everything in between—and give students a candid behind-the-scenes look at what it's really like to build a creative career. These are the strategies that they will need to one day achieve their goals and to sustain them or help them shift strategy when things aren't working.

My guests' careers are quite diverse, but the creative and business processes they describe are often strikingly similar. Whether they've founded a start-up, created a niche as a visual artist, or became famous for their unique, disruptive ideas, their cumulative advice reveals patterns—universal protocols and best practices for making a living with your ideas. I recognized the same patterns in my own journey.

Everything I've experienced informed what I did next. The skills I used as a designer translated directly into the film industry. I had to come up with a creative idea, be able to communicate it clearly to others, figure out the labor and materials needed, cost it out, and be able to sell the product at a profit. I had wrestled in high school and college and always had to think a few moves ahead and be able to pivot quickly when meeting resistance. Business was no different.

The conversations with the guests in my class, and my experiences, gave me insight into what it takes to build and sustain all different types of creative careers. Over the course of our thirty-five-year relationship, I've learned invaluable lessons from Ralph Lauren about how to build a global brand. But I've learned just as much from the people I've interviewed who run small companies or have found a way to simply earn a living doing what they love.

When people started telling me how much they wished they'd taken a course like Creative Careers, I began looking for books that shared a similar range of advice but came up empty-handed. There are plenty of books about how to succeed in business and several on finding inspiration and expressing yourself as an artist, but I couldn't find any that taught readers how to balance business and creativity so they could earn a living doing what they love. In trying to sell this book, many publishers asked why a businessperson would buy a book about creativity, or they wondered why a creative person would want a book about business. They totally missed the point.

This is information that can benefit anyone, whether their goal is to be an entrepreneur or a creative, someone looking to make a career change, or an executive who works with creatives. For too long, our culture has subscribed to the myth that some people are simply good at business, while others are creative—not both. Wrong. Look at brilliant and creative businesspeople such as Elon Musk, Oprah Winfrey, Steven Spielberg, Kathy Ireland, and Stephen King.

Even the most dedicated artists spend up to 80 percent of their time on the business side of their careers. Knowledge about business is crucial to their survival, but art schools rarely teach business. And separating people into "business" and "creative" silos is equally unfair to those with a head for business who aren't taught or encouraged to express themselves creatively.

Using stories and advice from my class guests, my own career, and the dozens of creative leaders I've interviewed outside of the classroom, I will teach readers how to access their creativity by discovering what creativity really is, how they personally define success, how to overcome fear and doubt, and how to feed their natural creativity. We will focus on identifying opportunities, evaluating an idea's potential, and capturing the market's attention. The reader will learn how to make a living with those creative ideas by assessing risk, finding the right collaborators, and ultimately building an effective and meaningful personal brand.

My students are constantly encouraged to ask questions as a means of finding their own voices. In that spirit, each part of the book will be structured around the questions I ask my class guests and questions for the reader to ask him- or herself. The result will be like listening in on candid conversations with some of the most successful artists and entrepreneurs in the world, all while conducting a self-exploration that will help readers discover what they really want out of a creative career and, ultimately, how to get it.

THE PEOPLE
YOU'LL BE HEARING FROM

MICHAEL ARAD is the architect and designer of the National September 11 Memorial at the World Trade Center site, titled Reflecting Absence, which was selected by the Lower Manhattan Development Corporation from among more than five thousand entries submitted in an international competition held in 2003.

DAVE ASPREY is the founder of Bulletproof and author of *New York Times* best sellers *The Bulletproof Diet* and *Super Human*. Dave is the creator of the widely popular Bulletproof Coffee; host of the number-one health podcast, *Bulletproof Radio*; and a Silicon Valley investor and technology entrepreneur.

TOM BILYEU is an entrepreneur known as a cofounder of Quest Nutrition, the second-fastest-growing private company in North America, on the *Inc.* 500 for 2014. Tom's new venture is Impact Theory, to help people develop the skills they will need to improve themselves and the world. Tom was named one of *Success* magazine's "Top 25 Influential People" in 2018.

MORAN CERF is a neuroscientist and business professor at the Kellogg School of Management and the neuroscience program at Northwestern University. His academic research uses methods from neuroscience to understand the underlying mechanisms of our psychology, behavioral changes, emotion, decision making, and dreams.

DORIE CLARK is a professor at Duke University's Fuqua School of Business and the author of *Entrepreneurial You*, *Reinventing You*, and *Stand Out*, which was named the number-one leadership book of 2015 by *Inc.* magazine. Dorie is a marketing strategy consultant, professional speaker, and frequent contributor to the *Harvard Business Review*.

RACHEL CRANE is an innovation and space reporter for CNN, creating original video content to be shown across CNN's platforms. She was honored to receive the NewSpace Journalism Award, given to an organization or individual for outstanding work in journalism.

DENNIS CROWLEY is cofounder and executive chairman of Foursquare, the technology platform that powers location experiences for more than 1 billion people around the world. Previously, he founded Dodgeball, one of the first location-based mobile social services (acquired by Google in 2005).

LAURA EDWARDS works with brands to help them define how they show up in culture. For the past five years, Laura worked at Adidas on global marketing strategy, specifically with sports, entertainment, and influencer partnerships.

SAVANNAH ENGEL offers fashion, consumer, and lifestyle brands a full menu of services, including marketing, communications, social media and brand-partnership consulting, as well as VIP and influencer relations and events. Savannah's experience in communications for fashion and entertainment has supported brands like Michael Kors and Barneys New York, plus musical artists such as Zayn Malik, Iggy Azalea, and Rita Ora.

MICAELA ERLANGER is a celebrity fashion stylist based out of New York City and Los Angeles, where she works with such international talent as Lupita Nyong'o, Jared Leto, Meryl Streep, Common, and Michelle Dockery. Her work has been seen on the most prestigious red carpets and in the pages of top fashion publications worldwide.

TIM FERRISS is an early-stage technology investor and adviser for Uber, Facebook, Shopify, Duolingo, Alibaba, and more than fifty other companies. He authored five number-one *New York Times* and *Wall Street Journal* best sellers, including *The 4-Hour Workweek*, which was translated into thirty-five languages. *The Tim Ferriss Show* podcast is the first business and interview podcast that has exceeded 400 million downloads. Tim serves on the advisory board of DonorsChoose.org, an educational nonprofit and the first charity to make the *Fast Company* list of "50 Most Innovative Companies in the World."

VANESSA FRIEDMAN is a fashion director and chief fashion critic for the *New York Times*. She leads global fashion coverage for both the *New York Times* and the *International New York Times*.

DANIEL GULATI is managing director of Comcast Ventures. Daniel is an early-stage venture capital (VC) investor focused on consumer companies. Daniel saw the potential in Away luggage and was their first investor.

FRAN HAUSER is a media executive, start-up investor, keynote speaker, and best-selling author of *The Myth of the Nice Girl*. Eighteen of the twenty companies in Hauser's investment portfolio are founded by women.

AMANDA HESSER is an entrepreneur, cofounder, and chief executive officer (CEO) of Food52. She was the food editor of the *New York Times Magazine* and author of *The Essential "New York Times" Cookbook*, a *New York Times* best seller.

SABIN HOWARD is a teacher and master sculptor, whose works are owned by museums and private collectors all over the world and have been shown at more than fifty solo and group shows. Sabin, along with architect Joe Weishaar, was selected as the winning design team for the National World War I Memorial in Washington, DC.

KATHLEEN IRELAND is an American model and actress turned author and entrepreneur. Ireland was a supermodel in the 1980s and 1990s, best known for appearing in thirteen consecutive *Sports Illustrated* swimsuit issues. In 1993, she founded kathy ireland® Worldwide, a multibillion-dollar worldwide brand marketing company that has made Ireland one of the richest self-made women in the world. Kathy is involved with various charities and nonprofit organizations dedicated to education, emergency response and training for children, disease research and management, and HIV/AIDS.

OLIVER JEFFERS is a visual artist and author working in painting, bookmaking, illustration, collage, performance, and sculpture. His critically acclaimed picture books have been translated into more than forty-five languages, and over 12 million copies have been sold worldwide.

DAYMOND JOHN is a businessman, investor, television personality, author, and motivational speaker. He is best known as the founder, president, and CEO of FUBU and appears as an investor on the ABC reality television series *Shark Tank*.

STEPHANIE JONES is CEO and founder of JONESWORKS, a full-service, strategy-driven public relations, marketing, and communications agency representing an elite roster of talent, fashion, lifestyle, beauty, and consumer brands.

KARLIE KLOSS is an American supermodel, forty-time *Vogue* cover girl, media star, entrepreneur, and philanthropist. Karlie was recognized on the *Time* 100 list for her philanthropic work as the founder of Kode with Klossy and was featured on the covers of *Fast Company* and *Forbes*.

STEVEN KOLB started his career working with nonprofits such as the American Cancer Society and the Design Industries Foundation Fighting AIDS organization. He had no background in fashion when he was hired by the Council of Fashion Designers of America (CFDA), the trade association for the American fashion industry, in 2006. In 2011 he became its chief executive.

SUSAN LACY is a documentary filmmaker known for creating *American Masters*, the acclaimed PBS biography series profiling artists and visionaries who have helped shape our country's culture. The series has seventy-one Emmy nominations and twenty-eight wins. Lacy directed and produced *Spielberg* and *Jane Fonda in Five Acts*, both for HBO Documentary Films. Both were nominated for Emmys.

DYLAN LAUREN is an entrepreneur and founder of Dylan's Candy Bar, which claims to be the "largest candy store in the world." She is the daughter of American fashion designer Ralph Lauren.

FREDDIE LEIBA created the then unknown career of fashion stylist. He was part of the team that launched *Interview with Andy Warhol*. Freddie served as creative director of *Harper's Bazaar* and contributed in various creative capacities to several Condé Nast titles around the world. He has worked with legendary photographers such as Richard Avedon, Irving Penn, and Helmut Newton. Freddie has styled Oscar winners and nominees Halle Berry, Cate Blanchett, Sandra Bullock, Jessica Lange, Julianne Moore, Julia Roberts, Meryl Streep, Kate Winslet, and Salma Hayek. He has worked on numerous national ad campaigns and designs the uniforms for many of Ian Schrager's hotels.

JON LEVY is a behavioral scientist and author who works in the fields of influence, community and customer engagement, and adventure. Levy founded the Influencers, a dining experience and community, whose participants include more than fourteen hundred leaders, ranging from Nobel laureates, Olympians, and celebrities to executives, editors in chief, and royalty.

DANIEL MARTIN is a New York–based makeup artist whose work has been featured in *Interview*, *Vanity Fair*, and *Harper's Bazaar*. Among his clients are Her Royal Highness, the Duchess of Sussex; Elisabeth Moss; Jessica Alba; and Jessica Biel. Daniel is currently a brand ambassador for Dior Beauty and the creative color consultant for Honest Beauty.

BRANDON MAXWELL established a styling career in 2012 acting as a fashion director to Lady Gaga. His luxury women's ready-to-wear label launched in New York in 2015. The brand is worn by Michelle Obama, Meghan Markle, Oprah Winfrey, Blake Lively, Jane Fonda, Queen Rania of Jordan, and Tiffany Haddish. Brandon was awarded the 2019 CFDA Award for "Womenswear Designer of the Year." He is a judge on the award-winning show *Project Runway*.

MAURA MCGREEVY is a communications executive with nearly twenty years of public relations (PR) and marketing experience spanning industries such as media, advertising, sports, fashion, technology, entertainment, and finance. A native of Moscow, Idaho, and graduate of Boston University, Maura now resides in New York City with her husband.

LEANDRA MEDINE is an author, blogger, and founder of Man Repeller, an independent fashion and lifestyle website that has more than 2.2 million followers. In 2012 Leandra was featured in *Forbes*'s "Top 30 Under 30" as one of the year's "most influential trendsetters."

DEBBIE MILLMAN was named "one of the most creative people in business" by *Fast Company* and "one of the most influential designers working today" by Graphic Design USA. Debbie is also an author, educator, curator, and host of the podcast *Design Matters*.

MONICA MITRO is executive vice president (EVP) of public relations at Victoria's Secret and co–executive producer of the *Victoria's Secret Fashion Show* holiday television special.

BEN PARR is an award-winning entrepreneur, investor, and journalist. Ben is the author of the best-selling book *Captivology: The Science of Capturing People's Attention*. He was named one of the top-ten tech journalists in the world by Say Media and one of the top-ten "Internet of things" experts by *Inc.* magazine.

JOE POLISH has utilized his marketing expertise to build thousands of businesses and generated hundreds of millions in profits for his clients, ranging from large corporations to small family-owned businesses. Joe leverages his networking prowess to bring together the top industry transformers and leaders in the world. He founded Genius Network and GeniusX, high-level marketing and business groups for industry transformers and leaders.

MAURO PORCINI is senior vice president and chief design officer at PepsiCo. Mauro is responsible for leading innovation by design across the company's food and beverage portfolio, extending from physical to virtual expressions of the brands, including product, packaging, events, retail activation, architecture, and digital media. Chosen as one of *Fast Company*'s most creative people in business.

AMBER RAE, called a "Millennial Motivator" by *Forbes*, speaks to audiences across the globe on topics ranging from navigating emotions to cultivating joy to unlocking creative potential and has collaborated with brands such as Kate Spade, Microsoft, TED, and Ogilvy. She is the author of the best seller *Choose Wonder over Worry*.

JOY-ANN REID is the host of *AM Joy*, a twice-weekly political talk show that airs weekend mornings on MSNBC. Joy serves as a political analyst, appearing on NBC News and MSNBC programs, including *Meet the Press*, *Hardball with Chris Matthews*, *The Rachel Maddow Show*, and *Andrea Mitchell Reports*.

JOSH SAPAN, one of the entertainment industry's most innovative executives, is responsible for the overall management of AMC Networks, known for its award-winning original content. The company consists of several leading entertainment brands, including national television networks AMC, BBC America, IFC, SundanceTV, and WE tv. Josh was honored by *Fast Company* as one of the "100 Most Creative People in Business."

YUKO SHIMIZU is an award-winning illustrator and professor of illustration at the School of Visual Arts (SVA). Yuko's work has been commissioned by Apple, Adobe, Microsoft, MTV, Target, National Public Radio, *Time*, the *New York Times*, the *New Yorker*, *Rolling Stone*, *GQ*, and many more.

SIMON SINEK is the author of multiple *New York Times* best-selling books. He is best known for popularizing the concept of WHY in his first TED Talk in 2009, which has had more than 40 million views.

SALLY SINGER is creative director at *Vogue* and former digital creative director of Vogue.com. Sally built *Vogue*'s online presence.

AMY SMILOVIC is founder, CEO, and designer of the Tibi fashion company. A former advertising exec who was with Amex, Amy had no formal training in fashion. Creativity was always her passion. Her mission is inspiring women to embrace and define modern femininity on their own terms.

HILLARY STERLING is partner and chef at the renowned New York City restaurant Vic's. While Hillary was earning a business degree from Indiana University, she began taking night classes at a local cooking school in Bloomington and discovered her passion: food. She is now considered one of New York's top chefs.

DAN SULLIVAN is founder and president of Strategic Coach, Inc. Dan has more than forty years' experience as a highly regarded speaker, consultant, strategic planner, and coach to entrepreneurial individuals and groups. Dan works to help entrepreneurs reach their full potential in both their business and their personal lives.

TERRY TSIOLIS was born and raised in Montreal and left for New York City to obtain a master's degree in communications. Terry worked under Fabien Baron and Liz Tilberis at *Harper's Bazaar*. He then pursued a career in fashion photography. His editorial credits include *Harper's Bazaar*, *Arena Hommes Plus*, the *Face*, *i-D*, *L'Uomo Vogue*, and *V*. His advertising clients include Anne Klein, Armani, Burberry, Byblos, Club Monaco, Cole Haan, DKNY, Dunhill, Eres, and J. Crew.

RYAN URBAN is CEO and cofounder of BounceX, one of the fastest-growing and most innovative behavioral marketing platforms in the world. Ryan helps businesses convert their website visitors into customers. Ryan was featured in "*Crain*'s 40 Under 40."

MAX VADUKUL is noted for his art reportage and portrait photography, which he describes as "taking reality and making it into art." He has a lifelong affinity with black-and-white photography, a foundation of much of his early work. His work has been seen in the *New Yorker*, *French Vogue*, *Italian Vogue*, *L'Uomo Vogue*, *W* magazine, *Interview*, *Rolling Stone*, and many other publications around the world.

ROY WOOD JR. is a comedian, writer, and correspondent on *The Daily Show*. Roy has performed around the country, starred in comedy specials, and been a guest on *Conan*, *The Tonight Show with Jimmy Fallon*, *Late Night with Seth Meyers*, and *The Late Show with Stephen Colbert*.

RANDI ZUCKERBERG is an entrepreneur, investor, best-selling author, award-winning producer, and founder and CEO of Zuckerberg Media. Passionate about the intersection of tech and media, Randi was an early employee at Facebook, where she was the creator of Facebook Live. Randi hosts a weekly tech business show called *Dot Complicated* on SiriusXM.

PART ONE

WHAT IS YOUR VISION?

1

The Myth of the Lightning Bolt

YEARS AGO, I WAS DIRECTING a commercial for Victoria's Secret and was working with the legendary Academy Award–winning cinematographer Vilmos Zsigmond. He shot *Deliverance*, *Close Encounters of the Third Kind*, *The Deer Hunter*, and many other great films. For a split second, there was a beautiful shimmering, like the reflection of water, on the wall of the set. I asked Vilmos if he saw that flash. He said it was caused by a crew member walking past one of the lights as he crossed the set carrying a sheet of Mylar. This was not the look we had planned, but I loved the shimmering light and scrapped the original lighting concept for the commercial and started over using the Mylar. The client loved it.

A fortunate accident led to success. All creatives have experienced fortunate mistakes or accidents that turned something unexpected into something wonderful. In movies and novels, we are told that great ideas simply come to us in a flash of inspiration. That's what I call the Myth of the Lightning Bolt. Creative ideas may seem to come out of nowhere, but they almost never do. You might experience a breakthrough that connects the dots, but those dots have been percolating for a while and you are finally seeing the relationships between them. Vilmos, as a result of his years of experience as a cinematographer, knew exactly what caused the look and how to replicate it. It's being prepared, alert, and ready that leads to that breakthrough, not something haphazard like luck.

There are a lot of misconceptions about creativity. For one, we often mistake technique for creativity. Technique is how you execute, not the creativity itself. An actor can have good technique and know how to use her voice and body but not bring any emotion or a unique perspective to her role. Technique without creativity gives you stock photography or Muzak, not something interesting or evocative.

Another misconception is that you must be a painter, writer, actor, dancer—someone in the arts—in order to have a creative career. A dentist developing a new drilling technique, a teacher finding a unique way to reach a troubled student, a coder, accountants, lawyers, or an entrepreneur starting a new business are all using their creativity to organize the information they are presented with to solve problems.

Ryan Urban is the CEO and founder of BounceX, a leading online behavioral marketing firm founded in 2012. The mission of BounceX is to identify a brand's consumers and provide the most relevant digital experience based on their behaviors. Ryan believes that even the language you use can either promote or stifle creativity and innovation. For example, the word *hope* is banned at BounceX because it doesn't stimulate creative thinking. Many companies *hope* that people will visit their sites and buy from them, but, as Ryan says, "Hope is not a business model."

Instead of hoping, Ryan did a deep dive into data and researched the online behavioral indicators of how and when people buy online. We have all left a lot of merchandise in the carts of online retailers. Converting a shopper into a buyer is a problem every retailer wants to solve. How do people shop online? When do they make the decision to buy? When should a seller offer a discount or suggest other merchandise? These are questions for online sellers. Using behavioral economics and algorithmic organizing principles, BounceX has substantially upped the conversion rate from shopper to buyer, generating millions of dollars for his clients.

The creative mind is always seeking new perspectives; it is passionately curious and hungry to solve problems. That's creativity at work.

WHAT FEEDS CREATIVE IDEAS?

How can you prepare to experience creative breakthroughs? Be aware. Be informed. Be engaged. Constantly educate yourself. Read. Go to concerts, movies, and plays. Talk to people. Ask questions.

Another time I was approached by Victoria's Secret to shoot a commercial for a gift with purchase—an umbrella—and asked if I had any ideas. I had just seen *Hamilton* on Broadway and was inspired to do something with music and choreography. I thought the umbrellas would be interesting shot from overhead, like a Busby Berkeley musical from the 1930s combined with modern dance movement. Shooting them from overhead was also a great way to show the product. I collaborated with Stephanie Klemons, the associate choreographer of *Hamilton*. That resulted in the Victoria's Secret "Angels and Umbrellas" commercial, one of their most successful gift-with-purchase promotions.

You never know where inspiration will come from, what neurons will fire, to form an idea. It's important to constantly expose yourself to the best work out there. If I hadn't just seen the Broadway show, that idea might not have occurred.

Michael Arad
on Actively Imagining Another World

Michael Arad, the award-winning architect who designed the World Trade Center Memorial, says that architects and designers must actively imagine another world and be consumed by it, even if they don't necessarily think it's going to lead to a commission. Nothing is a waste of time if you use the experience wisely. When Michael created his proposal for the memorial, he chose to ignore the formal guidelines that were laid out for submission.

He was surprised when he won the competition. It was challenging from the beginning, but he had a strong vision for what he wanted to do and that is what kept him motivated:

I saw the plane crash into the South Tower and then saw how we came together. I wanted to reflect that in the work. If I had not experienced this personally, I wouldn't have had a desire to give as much thought and effort and consideration to understanding my feelings about the events of that day. It was a transformative moment.

I learned a lot through this process. Despite the significant changes, I feel that the design was true to itself, to those two core principles that I outlined: I wanted to make (the feeling of) absence the goal and try to make the memorial a public space. I saw how easily the memorial could have slipped into something completely different. It could have become very jingoistic, very aggrandizing or self-pitying. There are so many moments where it could have become an altogether different memorial and reflected a different set of emotions and beliefs and not what I was hoping to reflect, which is how New York got together.

Design is in some ways almost like a problem-solving exercise, like a riddle, but you're trying to find the answer with walls and windows and floors and materials and construction technology and the site—you're never done. There's always another iteration, another option, another way to try to solve it.

Michael noted the importance of being able to explain the logic behind what you are trying to put forth in a project.

It's important when it comes to getting other people to be part of the process for them to understand why something is important. Otherwise, it becomes capricious. Like, "Oh, I think it should be green. No, I think it should be blue." It should be for a reason and in support of a narrative. As a designer, it's like you're a writer.

From his initial concept, Michael crafted a narrative of absence; highlighting what was no longer there, the building and the lives that were lost on 9/11. He symbolized that loss in the memorial he designed. He wanted it set in an open space where people could gather and life would go on. These were all creative decisions involving many stakeholders and politicians as well as a lot of money. Michael communicated and defended the logic of his narrative. He faced a lot of opposition, but ultimately he succeeded. The World Trade Center Memorial is now considered a timeless masterpiece.

I was hired to produce a lifetime-achievement video for Ralph Lauren. A group of us were reviewing hundreds of images for inclusion in the video. The award was going to be presented to him at a black-tie event at Lincoln Center. There was a lot of conversation about other fashion designers who had been honored. Ralph looked at me and said, "You're being very quiet. What designer do you think I'm like?" I told him I think of him as more like Walt Disney than a fashion designer because it's not just about the fashion: "You create worlds with your work—just like Disney." Ralph smiled, pointing his finger at me, and replied, "You get it." Ralph says he writes through his clothes and uses the metaphor of "making a movie" for how he creates. Sometimes that movie is a western; sometimes it takes place on the French Riviera or on safari. Ralph Lauren creates wardrobes for the different roles that people play in their lives. It made perfect sense that he chose Audrey Hepburn, an Oscar-winning movie legend, to present him with the award.

Ralph says that when people get dressed, they act differently:

When a woman is buying something, she's dreaming; she is projecting her moods and her feelings—that's a sense of fun and excitement—like watching a movie. If I'm wearing a suit, I might take on the role of a CEO. When I wear jeans and cowboy boots, I have a different sensibility. We all have different moods, and clothes are a part of the mood. I always wanted to be an actor, so I think clothing has been my way of acting through the clothes.

The fashion industry is driven by desire. You see something wonderful; you want it. Growing up, Ralph was no different. Every day on his way home from school, he passed a store that had a very cool pair of blue suede shoes in the window. He wanted them. He couldn't afford them.

Ralph can now afford anything he wants, but he still has that same sort of desire for beautiful things that initially inspired him. His entire career is about creating those things.

Ralph did not come from money. His parents were Russian immigrants, and America represented the land of opportunity, reflected in the movies he loved and constantly watched when he was growing up. Movies became the organizing principle for how he approaches design. If he is doing safari clothes, he's creating a movie in that world. He imagines a character and decides this is what she would wear at night; this is what she would wear in the daytime. Movies, the stars, and their homes—Audrey Hepburn, Grace Kelly, Cary Grant, Paul Newman—have inspired a lifetime of desires and designs.

ORGANIZING PRINCIPLES

When I was in sixth grade, I got into an argument with my next-door neighbor Billy. His parents had gotten him a telescope for his birthday. We were in his backyard looking at the star-filled night sky.

"I see Orion," said Billy, looking through the telescope. He let me look and asked, "What do you see?"

"I see a bunch of stars."

"No, I aimed it at Orion. See him?"

"I see a bunch of stars."

"Don't you see his belt? His sword?"

Billy got more and more agitated. "Everybody knows that's Orion. I can't believe you can't see him."

"Everyone might *agree* it's Orion, but it's not actually Orion— it was just a bunch of stars until someone told a story about it and gave it meaning."

Billy didn't let me look through his telescope anymore. But it is just a bunch of stars, until someone identifies a shape or a pattern and what they see becomes accepted as that's what it is. The sky is a vast canvas. We have to focus on small sections to make any sense of it. The constellations are organizing principles.

When nineteenth-century sculptor Rodin was asked, "How do you take a two-ton block of marble and turn it into a woman?" he responded simply, "The work of art is already within the block of marble. I just chop off whatever isn't needed." Rodin was describing his organizing principle: making discriminating selections so whatever you create has the greatest possible impact. Rodin found the "constellation" in a vast piece of marble. Another word for that is *editing*, which is a crucial piece of every creative process.

In a painting, a song, a book, a film, or a clothing design, information is being organized as part of the creative process. How do you synthesize what you see, hear, feel, and experience? What do you highlight? Where do you draw the boundaries? How do you decide what goes in and what is left out?

Rachel Crane, the innovation and space reporter at CNN, shoots much more footage than ends up being part of her six-minute stories. In order to come up with six minutes on the air, she is usually shooting for three or four days. You need to have much more than will appear in the final piece so that you can choose the best content. For example, in TV there is "A roll" and "B roll." B roll is the footage that goes over the talking to illustrate what someone is saying, as opposed to A roll, which is on camera with sound synchronized. For her pieces, a lot of B roll is required.

Shooting with a crew on location costs a lot of money. There are hours of footage shot and then edited to produce a segment. The editing takes a long time because you get attached to your footage and making choices gets difficult. It ultimately takes a lot of back-and-forth to complete a piece.

It's the same in every business. There are budgets and limitations to be aware of. There are people that you have to get aligned with your project who can help move it forward. In order to do good work, there is a lot of prework to be done before you ever present an idea. If you're designing a line of clothing, it's the same as having six hours of footage that ends up lasting six minutes. You edit. Then you edit again. And again. It's the same when writing a book or play. It's in every art form.

When you develop your own organizing principles for the world around you, you are thinking creatively. Conformity, the opposing principle, is sometimes more highly valued because it's comfortable and nonthreatening. We look at the chaos out there and feel compelled to impose order on it, an order that someone else has already defined. But when you look at the world through that narrow conformist framework, you fail to push boundaries and engage with the larger world outside of that border.

How can you start seeing a woman in a block of marble? It comes down to exactly what we're doing in this book: questioning, allowing your mind to *wander* so that you can begin to *wonder*, upending assumptions, and seeing the world through a wider frame.

Tim Ferriss, the author of many books, including *The 4-Hour Workweek*, told me, "I find that if you're trying to connect ideas, you need to provide vacuums. For me, that will often be long forms of exercise, whether it's a two-hour walk or an hour of mindless lap swimming. I think that empty space is really critical." In other words, while he exercises, Tim's mind wanders . . . and he wonders. "To facilitate creativity, I try to ask better questions. Those better questions can sometimes be absurd: What if I do the opposite of best practices? What if I stop doing 90 percent of what my competitors do for the next week? What if I completely stopped using email and phone for the next seven days as an experiment? I think we are hard-wired to have rituals and routines, and those are very, very helpful, but it can be even more valuable to jolt yourself out of that temporarily." Tim is talking about widening his frame by asking questions and challenging norms—all crucial elements of creativity.

Susan Lacy on How to Tell a Story That Hasn't Been Told Before

Susan Lacy created the acclaimed PBS series *American Masters* and went on to continue winning Emmys for her films at HBO. She always wanted to be a journalist. Susan was the editor of her high school and college newspapers and wrote feature pieces and portraits. On the last day of school, the students were given a topic and had to write an essay. She chose to write the story about the last day of school through the eyes of the janitor. She won a national award for it. It's an important insight into the creative mind: How do you tell a story that hasn't been told before? How do you look at something that happens every day in a fresh way, and how do you look at that through somebody else's eyes and come up with a new idea? That was instinctual to her, but that's such an important thing because it's formative in terms of how she approaches her work.

So many of the subjects she has filmed are extremely well known, such as Jane Fonda, Steven Spielberg, and Bob Dylan. Bringing something new and fresh to tell a story that the audience is not already aware of is also about organizing principles.

Every single film has a totally different story. And I don't just mean the story of the artist, but the story of how you approach telling that story. Many of the people that we made films about had in fact not had films made about them. Steven Spielberg had never participated in a book or film about himself.

Jaws was a difficult shoot, and Spielberg started making films when he was a child. His fans know this. The whole world doesn't necessarily know it. I remember thinking, "How do I tell the story of Jaws, which a lot of people know, in a different way?" It came from Steven. He was so willing to talk about his fears as a filmmaker, so I ended up telling that story from his point of view, as a twenty-three-year-old making his first big movie. He had made one movie before, Sugarland Express, but this was a big movie, and he insisted on shooting on the open ocean, which nobody had ever done. Everything had always been done in a lake or water tank.

He said, "I can't create that level of fear if I'm not shooting on the ocean." It was him telling that story very dramatically to me, of his fear every day that he was going to get fired. He said, "I didn't know anything about tides or the sun or how that changed the shoot." It was Steven sharing his experience of making that film and what he learned, about trusting his instincts, and, of course, he had no idea that it was going to become the biggest hit of that time. There is a difference between reading that story and Steven Spielberg telling you that story on camera, because he was notoriously reluctant to be shot talking about himself.

From her award-winning high school essay to her award-winning documentaries, Susan's organizing principle is going to the source, be it the janitor of her high school or Steven Spielberg, and viewing the story that unfolds through the eyes of the main character. It works. Susan has been nominated for twenty-eight Emmy Awards, winning fourteen, plus numerous other awards.

Roy Wood Jr. has his own unique organizing principles as it relates to comedy. Before he does a TV special, he performs at a smaller comedy club and records it. He then critiques Roy on the video and makes editing decisions as he watches his own performance. He thinks that a comedian should be able to put most of their material into two buckets: "Who are you, and how do you feel about something?"

Roy oscillates between periods of creating new jokes and having a creative block. That's when he goes back to his old material. "If you hit a creative block where you can't come up with the new stuff, look at your old stuff. You are essentially collaborating with yourself. Figure out ways to change it, twist it, and then you have something that's better, or that process could beget an entirely new idea."

New ideas are what creativity is about, but those ideas don't happen in a bolt of lightning. There is a process. For some, their creative approach formed when they were young and they've been refining it ever since. For others, creativity is methodical, trial and error, constantly getting feedback, knowledge, and experience. And there are those who feel an emotional impact, a passion that propels them forward into new, uncharted territory.

Artist Zaria Forman literally goes into uncharted territory. NASA chose her to accompany them to document climate change and the melting glaciers in some of the most remote areas of the world. Her work is large-scale photorealistic paintings.

Zaria offers a moment in time for people to connect with these places that are really far away and fall in love with them in the way that she has. She draws the beautiful landscape, not the destruction that's happening. She wants to inspire people with beauty and make them feel hopeful, as opposed to devastated and paralyzed, which sometimes scary news reports can do to us. Her process starts with traveling to these places at the forefront of climate change. She takes thousands of photographs. Then in the studio, she works from both her memory of the experience and the photographs to make these large-scale compositions.

Zaria begins with a simple pencil sketch, the outline of the iceberg, the water line. She works with soft pastels; it's basically like charcoal. She will start by layering colors together and smudging them around with her fingers and palms to get the right tones and then work on the finer details on top of that.

Zaria often works straight from a photo. Every now and then, she'll change the shape of the ice a little bit or mix and match a couple of different images, just to create what feels like a balanced composition, but it's pretty rare that she does that. Ninety percent of the time, she depicts the exact landscape that she witnessed because she wants to stay true to what actually existed at that point in time.

Drawing is my way of expressing and the best way I am able to play a part in helping to solve the climate crisis. Time is infused in every part of my work. First, there is the split second when I snap a photograph, and when I'm on-site this can feel a bit frantic, especially when the light is illuminating the landscape magnificently. I sometimes take thousands of photos in under one hour, but I have to remind myself to put my camera down and to be present, in order to soak in the experience with my heart and my eyes, which is equally as important as capturing it with my camera.

Back in my studio, drawing allows me the time to revisit that moment, that split second when I took a photograph, and literally and figuratively draw it out over the course of several months. It's a treat to get the chance to explore the details and intricacies that I may not have noticed on-site. While drawing, I have a chance to revisit those landscapes and then to offer those moments I witnessed to viewers, so they can gaze at it as long as they wish.

THE CREATIVE PROCESS takes time, curiosity, discipline, persistence. There is no one way or right way. Discover your way. Creativity is rarely a bolt of lightning. That's a myth.

Workbook Questions

- Describe your approach to creativity: Have you been refining it since you were young? Are you methodical? Do emotion and passion drive your work? Ask yourself why.

- How would you categorize the approach of the people in this chapter?

- How can you organize information differently to widen your frame?

- What types of activities allow you to let your mind wander?

- What mistakes have you made that have led to new ideas?

- How can you get better at editing your creative projects?

2

Success on Your Own Terms

ALICE: "Would you tell me, please, which way I ought to go from here?"

THE CHESHIRE CAT: "That depends a good deal on where you want to get to."

ALICE: "I don't much care where."

THE CHESHIRE CAT: "Then it doesn't much matter which way you go."

ALICE: ". . . So long as I get somewhere."

THE CHESHIRE CAT: "Oh, you're sure to do that, if only you walk long enough."

—FROM *ALICE IN WONDERLAND*

BEFORE YOU START ON ANY journey, you need to know where you want to go and why you want to go, and you have to discover how you want to go there before you can draw the map. We all want the same things—to be safe, to be successful, and to be happy. But what makes you happy? How do you define success? Why do you define it that way? Discovering the true answers to those questions will help you get where you *really* want to go. That requires some digging.

DEFINING SUCCESS

At the beginning of every semester, I ask my students to define success. They almost always start out associating it with money. I push further and ask them whether they would consider themselves successful if they were making a lot of money doing a job they hated. Can you be successful and miserable at the same time? That's when the interesting discussion starts. There are different types of success, but only you can define what it looks like for you.

Where do you get your satisfaction? What excites and engages you? How are those things tied to your definition of success? For some, work is a means to make money, and they seek their fulfillment elsewhere. For others, work is where their fulfillment comes from.

When my first business went from being fun and fulfilling to a drag, I asked myself why. What happened? I was getting press and recognition as well as making money. The business was growing, but the part that was fun was shrinking. The things I didn't like doing became more and more of what I had to do as the business grew. I asked myself what success is, not because at twenty-four years old I had profound insight. Quite the contrary. I didn't know what was going on and had to look at why I wasn't happy. Asking these questions helped me focus on what I really wanted to do. What made me feel successful was feeling happy and engaged with what I was doing.

I know a lot of people who have, if measured by the metric of money, done extremely well. However, if measured by happiness, their account is empty.

I feel fortunate I asked myself this when I was young. I've met a lot of people who realized they should have asked themselves this question a lot sooner. You can't begin to build a successful career until you know how you define success. Otherwise, how will you know whether you're on the right track? There is no one answer. There is no right answer. Defining success is highly personal.

How Do You Define Success?

If you can find what is most meaningful to you and make your work about that, that's the most important thing to do. It can take years of work, possibly even a lifetime, in order to discover what that actually is, but it is necessary for success.

—ZARIA FORMAN

It's first of all being able to be very proud of what you have accomplished and what you did to get there. Sometimes the accomplishments aren't that great, but at least you can be proud that you put the effort in to get there. Also, success is being able to wake up early and do what you want to do every single day of your life.

—DAYMOND JOHN

Being able to enrich the lives of other people, be it family or friends or coworkers, to me that's success. I don't think you can put a number to that, fiscally speaking, but I think being respected for my craft by my peers and being able to help younger people figure it out, too, I think that's a very respectable place to land.

—ROY WOOD JR.

The journey is my success. I don't know if I will ever settle because I feel like so much of getting to where you want to go is the journey: the people you meet, the highs and lows of that path. At the end of the day, I'm lucky that I don't have to worry about rent anymore and how much money I have for dinner or lunch or whatever. When you get to that point, that's success.

—DANIEL MARTIN

Success is seeing an idea happen through hard work and through a lot of people coming together. Success is seeing your dreams realized.

—KARLIE KLOSS

It's when you're satisfied with something, when it feels right, when you know that you don't want to add to it. You don't want to change it.

—MICHAEL ARAD

I define success by the intimacy or relationship that I have with people. So the more people who are in my life that I feel are inspiring and interesting and contributing to different thinking, that's success for me.

—MORAN CERF

My own definition of success has evolved throughout my life. Success is having the freedom to pursue my various creative interests while saying no to things that don't interest me without suffering catastrophic consequences. My wife, Margaret Donohoe, had an experience in her career that exemplifies this. As a model in the 1980s, she was asked to be the woman for a Virginia Slims campaign. She said no. She did not want to play a role in marketing cigarettes. The ad agency assumed she was negotiating for a higher fee. They offered her more money; she still said no. They offered her even more. "I could afford to have the integrity to turn them down because I was a successful model and always working. I don't know if I would have had the same integrity if I had needed that money to pay rent."

In business, being able to choose your projects with your core values in mind is my definition of success. In life, the longevity and integrity of the relationships you build and maintain are the most important measures of success.

FIND YOUR PASSION?
FOLLOW YOUR PASSION?

Find your passion. Follow your passion. It sounds good until you think about it. What are you supposed to do? How do you find it? Is your passion a calling or a discovery?

When you are looking for something, it can take time to find or recognize it. Especially passion. It's like dating. You may go through a lot of people until you discover the person with whom you most strongly connect. Some people seem to know immediately; they feel the relationship was "meant to be." Some people never experience that feeling.

My first career was as a fashion designer. Although I built a business and had some success, I wasn't passionate about it. Passion didn't drive me; momentum did. I started a business. The business took off. I didn't ask myself whether this was what I was passionate about. I was too busy for that. I was fortunate to discover at a young age what I didn't want to do. The challenge is to discover what you *do* want to do.

How do we become who we are and end up where we end up? I find this question endlessly fascinating. The ways we think about ourselves, the decisions we make, are the clues that reveal the mysteries of our life. Award-winning graphic designer Debbie Millman told me about a clue to her life that was found in a box in the basement:

When I was growing up, I was living in a world that I perceived as a world of scarcity as opposed to abundance and didn't think that I could do much of anything. I didn't think I was smart enough, pretty enough, connected enough, rich enough, anything enough, to be able to be much of anything. I had very little guidance.

My mother moved from New York to Florida. She downsized considerably and gave me a box of things that she'd kept in her basement that I didn't even know she had. In it were wonderful things like my report cards from third grade and book reports with all this sort of swirly type with happy faces over the eyes and lots of hearts and things. I came across a drawing that I did when I was about eight years old.

When I looked at it I didn't have any recollection of drawing it, but I suddenly realized that at eight years old, without even realizing it, I had predicted my future. Had I known that that was going to be my future when I drew it, it would've saved me a lot of grief.

When I was a kid, I made a movie theater in the basement of my house. I would rent 8mm films: three cartoons and "the feature." The films were silent, so I borrowed my sister's portable stereo and found music for the soundtrack. I had a tape recorder, so I would record sound effects and then, by eye, synch it up with the film. I also designed posters that I'd put around the neighborhood. Every Saturday, twelve to fifteen kids would pay a quarter for the movies and another quarter for a bag of popcorn. The popcorn was the most profitable because my dad bought a large tin for the house, which I'd put into lunch bags and sell. It was great. No overhead. All profit. My dad wondered how we could go through so much popcorn. I had great fun doing this. Twenty years later, when I was listening to music for use in a film project I was directing, I realized that I was doing what I loved doing when I was a kid. No wonder I was so drawn to it—although now I don't sell popcorn.

The former head of Facebook marketing, chief executive officer (CEO) and founder of Zuckerberg Media Randi Zuckerberg had a deep love of theater since she was a child. However, she doesn't believe that everyone has a calling. She believes that more important than being passionate is understanding what's happening around you and how to apply your talents to how the world is changing. She did that when she came up with the idea for Facebook Live.

Randi could not have known the winding path of her life that would take her to Facebook. It didn't exist when she was younger. Since leaving Facebook, she had a part in a Broadway musical, *Rock of Ages*, and is on the board of the Lincoln Center for the Performing Arts. Ironically, Facebook Live allowed users to "perform" in front of a live audience, not so far from what Randi was passionate about since she was a kid.

She discussed the challenges of trying to fit into a difficult culture:

> I spent a lot of early years in my career trying to fit what I thought other people wanted me to be, suppressing the things about me that made me unique in order to fit into a world of Silicon Valley, fit into a world of men, fit into a world of tech.
>
> The arts and theater were so important to me, and I didn't do any of that for ten years because I thought in order to survive and thrive in Silicon Valley, you have to be heads down as an entrepreneur. I wish I could go back and tell young Randi that the things about me that were unique would be the things that would ultimately make me succeed in business. It wasn't until I stopped suppressing those things inside of me that I actually started inventing things that were great, that I did things I was proud of. So don't shelve the things that make you, you, for people who are never going to be pleased by you anyway.

WHOSE GOALS ARE YOU PURSUING?

Political pundit and host of *AM Joy* on MSNBC, Joy Reid had to confront what many of us have to deal with, defining our own goals and desires rather than living up to those of our parents. She says the advice she would give to her younger self is to do everything that she did but to start much earlier in following what she was passionate about:

> I wasted a lot of time trying to pursue premed because my family wanted me to be a doctor, or trying to pursue a corporate job because I knew my family would be proud if I was a success in corporate America, rather than just knowing that from the time I was in sixth grade, what I loved was politics and what I loved was media. I should have pursued that from the very beginning.

The relationship we have with our parents is powerful in terms of who we are and what we become. My parents were always supportive of whatever I did. They were always curious and loved hearing about what I was doing. They were also savvy businesspeople, so we could talk about business decisions, too. My father died before I could share some of the bigger things that I've done that I wish he could have seen. I met Ralph Lauren's parents after one of his shows. I wondered how they felt as they saw their son walk down the runway to the cheers of the crowd. I asked Ralph if seeing them in the audience was emotional for him.

> It is always emotional to deal with parents. I was close to my parents. My father was an artist, a man who had dreams but didn't fulfill them. I think he saw my success as a fulfillment. I saw that in his face. My mother was excited about me having success, but if I were a doctor or a teacher or a lawyer, she would have been happier.

FOR MANY PARENTS, what their children want to do is a mystery—especially if they have chosen a career in the arts. Makeup artist Daniel Martin had a career that his parents didn't even know existed:

> It took my parents a long time to understand what I did. You do what? You go to their house and do makeup? It wasn't until my dad saw an article in a magazine about my career that he understood. "Oh, okay this makes sense now." Up until that point, I don't want to say that I felt like I failed, but I felt like in my parents' eyes I wasn't leveraging out for them. You want that validation from your parents, but then you don't want them to know that you need that validation.

Senior vice president and chief design officer for PepsiCo, Mauro Porcini sees something he finds troubling regarding the pursuit of success:

> I see too many young people—it's all about making money. The reality is that very few people will be able to have what we define as success or make a lot of money. If your goal is that, the vast majority of you are screwed. But if your goal is culture, is self-realization and self-expression, then there is a very high probability that you will succeed if you go for it.
>
> You need to leverage all the assets that you have—networking is part of it, and business is part of it—but the intent needs to be that naive, positive dream. That's because there are so many roadblocks. It's very, very tough, but if you are energized by your dream, then it is fun and you will reach your results.

Comedian and *The Daily Show* correspondent Roy Wood Jr. had to constantly protect himself from the negativity that can make the inevitable struggles even more difficult. The negative voices are often those around you who are having trouble fulfilling their own dreams and seek to bring down those around them to validate their own lack of success.

> Don't let anybody pollute your dreams. I let too many people make me believe I might not be able to do comedy. I'd get paired up on the road with a comedian for a week, and when you are the opening act, you're also the driver, going from city to city. I was in the car with these people who are talking themselves out of really being courageous and taking risks. Some of that rubbed off on me and made me more hesitant about taking chances. I wish I'd have gotten negative people out of my life sooner.

KARLIE KLOSS'S CAREER took off very fast. She uses her successful modeling career as a platform for other businesses that are both philanthropic and profitable. Models are in a unique position when they are starting out. They're young. They're a lot like actors or professional athletes. They are scouted and signed in many cases before they are old enough to sign for themselves. They have a relatively small window of active time compared to most careers. The smart ones use their exposure to parlay other opportunities. However, when they are starting out as young as Karlie, they need, at the very least, their parents' permission to pursue their career.

Karlie Kloss on Going for It

As a young model, to break through you really have to have the support of a major photographer, a major designer, or a major campaign. Somebody has to get behind you and say, this is "the girl."

When the fashion industry gets excited about someone—I couldn't say, "I'm going to do school, and I'll see you in June when school's out." It would have been over like that. I ran with it.

I'd never been to Europe. I'd never even left the country. I said, "Mom, we're going to Florence. We have to go meet Frida Giannini from Gucci. She wants to work with me on her collection. She wants me to be an exclusive and be the breakout of her show."

I have a lot of friends [from high school], and they're still my good friends to this day, mainly because they didn't really know what I did. For the majority of my high school career, the only work that they ever saw of mine was the cover of Teen Vogue in 2008. They didn't read Vogue, and they definitely did not read Italian Vogue. But they supported me. They knew I disappeared for weeks at a time or a whole month for the fashion collections, but they didn't really get it. It was better that way because they cared about me for who I was.

Had I not had the normal high school life, normal friends, normal family, I don't think I would be who I am today. A huge reason for my success is simply because I am who I am, which I hope is somebody who's grateful and humble and not affected by any of this.

THE FOUR FREEDOMS

I'm an entrepreneur, not because I thought I'd make a fortune. More than money, I value the freedom to do what I want to do. The freedom to express, the freedom to say no, the freedom to spend my time doing what I want to do are massively important to me.

The "Four Freedoms" sounds like a musical group from the sixties, but it's not. It's a philosophy essential to Dan Sullivan, CEO and founder of Strategic Coach, who works with high-net worth entrepreneurs. Through his work, he has gained great insight into what he thinks is essential for success.

Dan Sullivan's Four Freedoms

A lot of people think that money is at the heart of all entrepreneurial striving, but it's actually freedom.

The biggest freedom is freedom of time. Freedom of time when you are working means that you get to do the things that you have a tremendous passion for. It's what fascinates and motivates you forever. You want freedom from activities that aren't motivating to you. It has to do with more time not connected to work. In your midthirties you start wanting the free time, especially because family becomes an issue. You may have outside interests that you are deeply involved in, and you want that freedom of time. The freedom is that you can be doing those activities and not thinking that you should be working.

To get that kind of freedom and then be making increasingly larger incomes costs a lot of money. You have to pay money to make money. The money part of it is a means of getting the freedom. You want the way you are making your money to be of a higher and higher quality. You want to be working with customers and clients who inspire, who continually provide you with a challenge, who appreciate you and reward you with things other than money. They reward by referring you. The other thing is that you are always learning.

Then there's freedom of relationship. Day in and day out, I want to be surrounded by people I really like, who really stimulate me. If I am working with people that I don't learn anything from, I'll get out of it very quickly.

I've got three freedoms now. I've got freedom of time, freedom of money, freedom of relationship, but the big thing is the fourth: freedom of purpose. My purpose is to have a future that's always bigger than my past.

HAVING SUCCESS ON your own terms means you have to define what "your own terms" are. It's not easy. If you have a primary relationship, be it married or with a partner, if you have children, things will change. Your terms will change. Maybe free time changes to mean having the time to spend with your kids. As you get older, you may not want to do things you were willing to do when you were younger, like pulling all-nighters or working late or partying late all the time. Concerns about money may become less or more depending on how your life unfolds. There is the theory of life called "shit happens." For most of us, it's a roller-coaster ride. Whether your business is small or large, you face the same struggles. What is it you want to achieve? Financial independence? Creative expression? Emotional fulfillment? All the above?

When I was a kid, there was a juggler who I was totally fascinated by on *The Ed Sullivan Show*. He had seven plates he would balance by spinning them on seven sticks. By the time he got to the fourth one, the first one would be wobbling, and he'd have to run over to it, rotate the stick, then give the second plate a few spins, and then run down and get the fifth one going. As soon as he got that going, he'd have to run back to the third and fourth, which were about to fall, pay attention to them, and then run down and get the sixth one spinning. I don't know if the seven plates were intended to represent the seven days of the week, but they did to me. I saw this guy trying to move with great speed and efficiency trying to get all seven plates spinning at once. It was a lot of work and took a lot of skill, and spinning seven plates at once lasted for a brief moment. Ultimately, it was a futile effort. What the juggler was trying to do struck me as profound. His activity stuck with me as a metaphor for life: you stop paying attention, and things will fall apart.

Workbook Questions

- Do you relate to any of the definitions of success in this chapter? Whose and why?

- What is success for you?

- What are your core values?

- What can you do to align your creative pursuits with your values?

- If you made a lot of money doing something you hated, would you consider yourself a success? Why or why not? Remember, we're talking about making a lot of money—even though you hate what you do.

- What did you love doing when you were a kid?

- When do you feel the most connected and engaged with what you are doing?

- Do you feel supported in your efforts by friends or family?

- How is that support expressed?

- What does freedom mean to you on a personal level?

3

Where Is There White Space?

IN ANY INDUSTRY OR ENDEAVOR, there are unmet and unrecognized needs and desires, spaces that have yet to be filled. I call this the "white space." Discovering it can lead to innovative opportunities for creating products and services that don't yet exist.

Uber found the white space for personal transportation that could not have existed prior to the technology of GPS and smart phones. They saw the opportunity to connect those two technologies and create a revolutionary new business.

Netflix found the white space in movie and television entertainment, evolving from mailing DVDs to streaming video once that technology was ubiquitous, forever changing the media landscape.

Merging two disparate business models, the way men rent tuxedos for special occasions coupled with Netflix making the picking, shipping, and returning of movies easy, inspired the founders of Rent the Runway.

The retail real-estate market found white space by creating opportunities for pop-up stores that changed how products can be offered and tested to the consumer public without the tremendous risk of the ongoing overhead of a store.

WeWork saw that small businesses had a problem finding space without long-term commitments. They solved a problem and disrupted the office-space market.

Airbnb disrupted the hospitality industry along with creating income opportunities for people who previously would have never thought of renting out their home or apartment. Recognizing an opportunity, the white space, is an important talent in business and a critical talent for entrepreneurs.

CONNECTING THE DOTS

I'm an entrepreneur because I'm unemployable. Most entrepreneurs are. We have an idea for something we want to do and are compelled to do it. Taking direction from others can be frustrating and difficult if you have a desire to "think different," as Apple declared in their first commercial.

When I was in my first career as a fashion designer, I knew nothing about designing or manufacturing clothes. What I did know was that there was very little fashion out there that appealed to me or my contemporaries, the "baby boomers." We were the largest emerging consumer market. We were also an underserved market. We didn't want to dress like we were in high school, nor did we want to dress like our parents. Change was coming. Others recognized the opportunity, and contemporary clothing became a huge part of the fashion and retail industries.

When I was transitioning in my career, there were news and sports magazines that were well represented on television. Fashion magazines occupied a large percentage of the real estate on magazine racks, but had almost no representation on television. When I made the transition, I saw there was a great opportunity for fashion video production. Now it's everywhere. Looking back, I can place both of those opportunities in the context of "white space," or "a business opportunity." However, back then, it wasn't that I was so calculated or savvy about business. I was seduced by the possibility of creating a business that I thought would be a creative career and fun. I don't know if recognizing an opportunity is a talent, a skill, or both, but I know it's of critical importance in terms of having a creative career.

What Is an Entrepreneur?

An entrepreneur is someone who creates, builds, and seizes on a pain point or an opportunity and figures out a great product or service to address it.

—FRAN HAUSER

True entrepreneurs really are able to get successful results without being hindered by current limitations of resources. They just find a way.

—KATHY IRELAND, CHAIR, CEO, AND CHIEF DESIGNER
OF KATHY IRELAND® WORLDWIDE

An entrepreneur is someone who's a little bit crazy because you have to be crazy in order to look at all the millions of businesses that exist out there and think that only you have what it takes to create the millionth and one business. It's someone who loves taking risks, who's deeply passionate about solving a particular problem, and who has the charisma, the intelligence, the leadership to get other people to rally around that vision also.

—RANDI ZUCKERBERG

Someone who believes their ideas are worth being put into practice.

—LEANDRA MEDINE

Someone who is slightly delusional.

—AMY SMILOVIC

It's a mind-set that is more tolerant of risk and is in love with an idea to the point where they're willing to sacrifice a lot. People tell you that it's a bad idea and it's risky. Those are the three things that humans hate: sacrifice, risk, bad feedback—we don't like those things. An entrepreneur is a person who can overcome this. You create a mind-set by saying, "I don't care. I'm going to see the light at the end of the tunnel despite all the things that the immediate world suggests are not good for us."

—MORAN CERF

An individual who takes his or her destiny into their own hands. It's a person who when the scorecard comes down at the end of the year or end of their life, they know that they tried and made their best effort for it, and they don't make any excuses for it. That's an entrepreneur.

—DAYMOND JOHN

An entrepreneur is not just a term—it's a way of life. It's important to take a serious look at whether that lifestyle is appealing to you. There are pros and cons. If wage security, defined work hours, and benefits are important, it may not be desirable. If you value stability, entrepreneurship may not be the right choice. If you are passionate about your pursuit, if you can tolerate the roller-coaster ride emotionally and financially, are prepared to put in the time and whatever work necessary to keep it going, you might be most rewarded by having your own business. Only you can answer those questions, and it takes a deep, honest look at who you are to answer it.

Tom Bilyeu cofounded Quest Nutrition in 2010 with Ron Penna and Mike Osborn. The company grew by 57,000 percent in its first three years and was ranked second on the *Inc.* 500 fastest-growing companies in the United States in 2014. Quest is a model for many start-ups, in terms of their extraordinary growth in such a short amount of time. Mythology often surrounds entrepreneurship and fuels misconceptions about what it takes to be successful. Many people think, "Wow, they just rode that rocket ship to the stars." It's not easy. Bilyeu elaborates:

> It's important for young entrepreneurs to understand: it's going to be hard. Every employee that interviewed at our company, I used to give a speech that we called "The Dark Days Speech." It was basically, look, dark days are coming for you. It's the second law of thermodynamics. The world moves toward entropy. Things move toward chaos. That is the nature of things. You're never going to go on a vacation and come back and your room is put back together, right? It's not going to be cleaner than when you left; it's going to be messier.
>
> If you know that things move toward chaos, if you know that hard times are coming for you, then you've got to have something in you. Some reason, some mission, some something deep inside you—some people call it a passion. That passion is driving you to gain the skills that you're going to need to gain the mentality and the vision of who you are as a human being to push through that, to get to the other side somehow, some way. That to me is where you find success, when you can push through the difficulties.
>
> For successful entrepreneurs, it's not that things weren't hard; it's not that they weren't scared. It's just that you believe in something enough to keep fighting for it.

ARTIST ZARIA FORMAN'S work is photorealistic paintings of remote and exotic places. Her goal is to create an emotional connection between what the viewer sees and feels. She has traveled to faraway places with NASA to photograph and then paint images of the changing environmental landscape. When she was a child, she traveled with her parents for a month every summer. At first, they traveled out west, but then, when she was ten, they started leaving the country for places like Morocco, India, Bali, and Turkey. Her mother was a photographer who loved shooting in exotic places. Her father was a neuro-opthamologist who studied issues about the connections between the brain and the eye. What she does now is a combination of what her mother and father did, combining science and the beauty of exotic landscapes. That's white space.

Amanda Hesser had a stable job with a guaranteed wage, benefits, and the prestige that comes with being a writer for the *New York Times*. She was middle-aged and had two-year-old twins. The country was in recession when she decided to start her company. Those things didn't stop her. She was determined to figure it out.

Amanda, along with her business partner, Merrill Stubbs, cofounded Food52 in 2009. It's an interesting business model; the e-commerce makes up two-thirds of the revenue, with the remainder coming from advertising, including both display and brand partnerships. There is also a magazine that was reimagined online. It is an innovative company that has built a large, loyal, and enthusiastic community of home cooks that increases year after year. Their rapidly growing e-commerce shop appeals to an audience of more than 13 million people. The store now offers more than two thousand items. Amanda and Merrill have curated and grown the online shop through careful use of sales data, expanding at the high-volume category. This very modern company has very old roots.

Amanda Hesser
on Reinventing the Tried-and-True

I was a staff writer and editor at the New York Times *for eleven years. I did a lot of different things, including writing a couple of books. My last book was* The Essential "New York Times" Cookbook *in 2010. The* Times *hadn't done a classic best-selling cookbook since* The "New York Times" Cookbook *by Craig Claiborne in the sixties.*

It felt like another assignment, but once I got started, I realized that the New York Times *had been writing about food since 1850, not 1960, and the nineteenth-century archives were really deep and interesting and had not been uncovered. There was a bigger story for me to write about, and that was exciting to me. I took this on not realizing that it would be a five-year project. I was doing this at night and on weekends, in addition to my very busy full-time job at the* Times. *I was looking to hire someone to help me out with the recipe testing and the research. A colleague of mine said, "My friend Merrill is moving back to New York, and she went to cooking school."*

We instantly connected and started working on this. Over the course of five years, we cooked more than fourteen hundred recipes together and became good friends. We were constantly talking about what was happening in the food world.

The digital business that we now run was inspired by the New York Times' *nineteenth-century archives, and almost all of the food content was crowdsourced. There were power users, just like you might see on a website; they just happened to handwrite into the newspaper and get their work published. They were opinionated. It felt fresh. This behavior that we assume was born in the digital age actually wasn't at all. It's human nature. People want to be heard. They're searching for community. There are experts everywhere— they just need a platform. That insight, along with the fact that traditional media models were not working, made us realize there needed to be a new way. The observation that drove a large part of the business is that Merrill and I as consumers felt ungratified and not served well.*

> *As people who are passionate about food, cooking, and home, we didn't feel like there was a place where we could find inspiration, meet other people, learn new things, discover products, and have this world we could depend on and that would grow with us. The beauty of technology is that it can provide this kind of world in a way that wasn't possible before. The* Times *having crowdsourced content was great, but it didn't have the multidimensional service that you can have with a digital company. These various influences started us on the path toward building this company. I'm a natural risk taker, so it wasn't a fraught decision.*
>
> *As a journalist, my job is to connect the dots for people to see what's happening and what's coming. It came very naturally for us to think of the world in this way, and it has helped us in business because it's our way of thinking, to always be looking to connect the dots and to think of what's next.*

Amanda and Merrill looked at something that was 160 years old and realized something old could be reinvented to be new. The *New York Times* crowdsourced recipes back then. They reimagined it with new technology to create a modern online business. The dynamics of getting people together, establishing a community around a common interest, in this case food, is timeless. They saw the white space and were able to create a thriving business.

Getting yourself into a creative mind-set will help generate ideas, but to build and sustain a creative career, it's essential to learn how to evaluate your idea's potential. Find white space in the market that you can fill and use your ideas to garner the most precious commodity out there—attention.

It's also about being an eternal student: being curious, attentive, engaged, and always learning. That's the only way you even have the possibility to see those insights, connect the dots, and recognize the opportunity.

KNOW WHAT IDEAS HAVE VALUE

William Faulkner famously said, "In writing, it is important to kill your darlings." This applies not only to writing but to any type of creative endeavor. As a creative, you are always prospecting, panning for the gold that has value and eliminating everything else. Editing is the essential talent. As a designer, you must get rid of the outfit you love but doesn't fit with the collection you're presenting. As a merchandiser, it's the same process: finding which products work best together. As a photographer, it's what's in the frame. As a writer, it means cutting every word that doesn't either reveal character or move the plot forward.

Roy Wood Jr. goes through a rigorous process of editing when putting together a routine. Nothing can be precious.

> Your creations are not your children. We treat them like our children. We don't want anybody to talk bad about them. We don't want you to find a flaw in them. You're proud of it because you created this thing, but they're not your children, which makes it easier to cut them out of your life if things go wrong. Don't grow attached, but if it's something that you really believe in, and you're ready to roll the dice on it, roll the dice. When you do Colbert or Fallon, they give you four and a half minutes. If you turn in a six-minute set, you have to chop ninety seconds, or you do not get on TV that night. Find the ninety seconds. I don't care how much you like the joke. I don't care how much people laugh at it. It's got to go. Just do it and move on.

IF YOU DON'T let go of ideas that don't add value to the whole, you will end up wasting a lot of creative energy defending ideas that are not going to go anyplace. That doesn't mean that you don't stand up and advocate for what you think is important, but you also have to realize when to let go.

Whether you make a living selling clothing or cosmetics, telling jokes, or pitching a new business idea, you have to keep focused and have clarity about the decisions you make. A great deal of creativity is problem solving, so how do you think about what you need to think about in order to reach the best conclusions? Neuroscientist and professor at the Kellogg School of Management, Northwestern University, Moran Cerf tells us how we can optimize our brains to work more creatively and effectively.

Moran Cerf
on Coming Up with Ideas

One of the definitions of creativity that is popular among neuroscientists is changing the boundaries of your thinking and reframing your mind-set to see different perspectives.

There are moments when the brain is better at doing that and moments where the brain is less good at that. When you are sleeping, if you get to stage four (REM: rapid eye movement), the dream stage, you will rewire the brain so that as soon as you wake up, you are able, for a little while, to think about things from a different perspective.

One of the methods that neuroscientists are trying is to have a person who is trying to come up with an idea take a nap for ninety minutes. Make sure that he or she gets to stage four, the dream stage, and wake them up immediately after and ask them to try to solve the same problem you had before. People actually have immediately different ways about thinking about the same problem just because they had a chance to give their brain a moment to think about it from a different perspective.

Each individual has what we call a brain profile. This allows us to learn what your optimal state of thinking is. For some people, their best state of thinking is from 8:00 a.m. to 10:00 a.m. Another person may at their best state from 6:00 p.m. to 7:00 p.m. There's a person who thinks best right before a deadline and another who does things much earlier. Some people do their best collaborating, while others do best when they work alone.

There is no right answer. Every person has a different brain pattern. We can start mapping each person's brain and learning what is their optimum state: "For you, it's 8:00 a.m. when you're alone, just before the deadline. For you, it's 6:00 p.m. when you're hungry, and you're a bit depressed: that's your best poetry moment." Neuroscientists have the tools to help you find the optimum time and way to do something. Creativity is the first thing people look at.

The question is, how can I become the most creative version of myself based on the science of the brain? Moran believes we can all be creative, that our brains have the capacity to do things well beyond what we think. Although the brain is not a muscle and is much more complex, if you train it, it gets better at doing things. There are things you can do to enhance creative performance without having electrodes implanted in your head.

Moran suggests the simplest way to do it is to keep a diary. For the next week, start writing decisions you made during the regular day-to-day moments of your life and note what the conditions were when you made them.

Let's say you're going to go to lunch and you're going to have three items on the menu, steak, salmon, and salad, and you say, "Here's a choice. I want to eat, I had those options, and I chose the steak. I was hungry, and I felt that I needed vitamin B-12." Write it down; don't judge.

A friend says, "Let's go to the park," but you also have assignments to do. You think about it and then go to the park. Write "I had these choices, and I made this choice." Write as many decisions as you can. It's tedious, but write the choices! The food you ate and the way you chose to spend your time. Big choices and small choices.

At the end of the week, look at the diary and then mark which ones you feel you made the right choice and which ones you did not. "The salmon I chose, good choice." Highlight in yellow. The park choice, not a good idea. Black mark. Start writing them, and see how many good and bad choices you make. The key thing is trying to see what state you were in when you made a choice that you liked and the ones you didn't like.

> *You will learn that there are consistent traits that happen when you make choices that you like and not. Maybe you were stressed. Maybe you were hungry. Maybe it was the same time of the day. You will start seeing patterns. With neuroscience, we actually look at the brain in the same format, but we also try to see how your brain looks. We say, "Okay, this is your brain state in creative states. This is your brain state in noncreative states." If your brain isn't wired, there will be less data, but you will see the consistency. That's the best, easiest way to do it.*

We live in a data-driven world. Companies gather it, create profiles, and learn who you are, what your preferences are, and when and what you are likely to buy. You can track your experiences to learn about yourself. Instead of Facebook targeting you with ads and figuring out when you are more likely to buy, you can do it yourself and become aware when it's more likely that you would do something you don't want to do and change that.

Changing our perspective and looking at things differently can manifest in surprising ways. Rick Smolan, an award-winning photographer who is best known as the cocreator of the best-selling Day in the Life book series, told me that for years, radar operators around airports had been trying to filter the noise from birds and bats from their radar so they could better hear the planes and weather patterns. None of their colleagues thought that this feature had value; it was just a problem to solve. When a group of scientists heard about this, they realized, "You've got fifteen years' worth of bat migration data, and you've been throwing it away. Are you crazy?" The old saying "One man's dirt is another man's garden" is a great example as to how perspective can change the perception of value.

The sculptor Rodin said, "I invent nothing. I rediscover." Steve Jobs could have but wouldn't have said the same thing. Jobs was a brilliant brand marketer and wanted the public to believe Apple originated every product they sold. He was extraordinarily successful, which means there are always plenty of new opportunities. How will you know when you've found the right one?

SOLVE A PROBLEM

Dennis Crowley, the founder of Dodgeball and Foursquare, went to market with his idea, even though the technology for it to function properly didn't exist yet. Start-ups call this MVP, minimum viable product. Make something and put it out there. See if it works. Let people play with it. If it works, great. You may be on to something. Get it out there. If it doesn't work, fix it and make it better.

Dennis Crowley
on Getting It Right

We started Foursquare so I could figure out where all my grad buddies were so I could meet them for drinks after work. It was much easier than texting ten people, "Where you at? Where you at?" We've built technology that can help us understand where the devices are; there's this whole other business that I could have never imagined ten years ago. If I went back in time, Back to the Future *style, and said, "Hey, Dennis. This little grad school project is going to turn into this thing that can predict the number of phones that will be sold," I would never believe it, but that's just the way things work.*

Foursquare sold data to Wall Street based on their accurate predictions of iPhone sales. They were able to apply their data capture to help McDonald's with their "all-day breakfast." Chipotle hired them to determine viable new locations in Austin rather than relying on zip code data from five years ago. What Dennis discovered is their data is valuable in ways he never imagined. Dennis found the bat data.

The point is, if you spend three months building something and it turns out that it sucks, you just wasted three months. Hack these things together pretty quickly, and then just iterate on top of them. When we were at grad school at New York University (NYU), this is what we were doing every week. Make a project. You have to show it on Friday. That's the deadline. You don't have three months to build something. You make it. If it's good, you might bring it on to the next week. If it's not, you junk it and start with another project the next week.

We were in this mind-set at NYU of just churning through. You have four classes. There are four projects due every week. You're just churning out work. You have to prioritize between what you want to keep working on and what you don't.

There are two schools of thought. One is getting it out there. Fast. First. Iterate. The other is, get it right before you take it to market because you have one chance to make that first impression.

An established company like Facebook or Google polishes their work before they publish it or share it, as they should. Everyone is watching what they do all the time. If you're just two people working around your kitchen table or it's a student project, then just get it together and push it out there. The most important feedback you can get early on is whether people even get it. "What am I supposed to do with this thing? Why would I ever use this? I don't understand how it works. I would never use it." That's the type of feedback that you're looking for. It doesn't have to be designed or polished.

One of the biggest fears of creatives is that somebody will steal their idea. There is a strong tendency to be secretive and not share. Another big fear is not knowing when to let go of your work and just release it.

I meet so many people who don't want to share the ideas that they have. They're like, "I can't possibly tell you what I'm working on because you're going to steal the idea and run with it." I'm like, "I'm not going to steal your stupid idea," and at the same time it's like, who cares? There are a hundred people in the city who have the same idea. It matters: Can you build it or not?

The questions for all businesses are the same. Whether you are asking them to try a streaming service and see if they like it, an electric toothbrush, an app, or clothing, the big questions are as follows: Does anybody like this other than me? Does it somehow enhance your life? Make doing something easier or faster? Solve a problem? Sometimes a product has benefits not even anticipated by the company that offered it.

Workbook Questions

- 💡 What does *entrepreneur* mean to you?

- 💡 What are the pros and cons of being an entrepreneur versus having a job?

- 💡 What quality-of-life aspects are most appealing to you and why (for example, freedom of time, learning new things, a steady income, health benefits)?

- 💡 Are there products or services missing from your life that could be a business opportunity?

- 💡 What problems interest you, and what solutions can you think of to create a business?

- 💡 What are the things you do that make you feel most excited and engaged?

- 💡 What ideas, products, or services are you passionate about?

PART TWO

GETTING OFF THE GROUND

4

Be Smart About Your Hustle

STUDY ART IN SCHOOL? GET a degree in an unrelated field as a backup plan? Skip school and learn by doing? There is no right or wrong answer, but by asking yourself the right questions, you can determine what is right for you.

ALWAYS BE LEARNING

You don't get an education—you take it. If you don't engage and put in the necessary work, you won't learn anything. Education doesn't stop once you leave school. Everyone who is great at what they do is constantly learning by being present and paying attention. I ask my guests, now that you are out in the world, what kind of course do you wish you would have taken that would have helped you in your career?

Painter Zaria Forman told me that "being an artist is running a business." I've interviewed a number of artists, none of whom learned anything about business in art school. You have to learn how to manage your money. It's very exciting when you get a big check. Money is the most fun when you spend it, but you have to save it for those times when you don't sell anything.

Artist, author, and illustrator Oliver Jeffers said:

A month after I graduated, I went into a small business course because nobody was teaching me how to do taxes or to write invoices or to keep on top of payments or anything like that. [In art school] there was a lot of technical information, there was a lot of conceptual information, but none of it was practical in the sense of being a functioning human being in the adult world rather than just a functioning artist.

Knowledge of business is like the martial arts: it's learning how to protect yourself so you can continue doing what you love doing. Daymond John took some hits before realizing the importance of business knowledge. He encourages everyone to go to college and study business or finance, regardless of their ambitions. He told me that his business ended up in jeopardy several times because of his own lack of financial intelligence.

No matter what, go to college. Learn business, learn accounting, and that's universal—no matter what. Even after I had made a large amount of money, I looked in the bank account, turned around, and it was half gone because of my lack of financial intelligence. It's really hard to make it, and it's ten times harder to keep it. I made a lot of mistakes until I really was able to get hold of it.

Karlie Kloss started her modeling career while she was in high school. Even with the tremendous success she's had, she sees continuing her education as essential. Karlie loves business. She took classes at NYU for venture capital (VC) and private equity. Her goal is not only starting but also investing in businesses, which she has done.

Randi Zuckerberg answered:

I wish that I would have taken a course on storytelling because everything about marketing, everything about starting a business, is how well you can tell your story, your personal brand. Can you tell your story in such a compelling way that other people want to get on board with it? That would have been much more useful to me than half the statistics classes I took.

A course in critical thinking is essential. How do you look at things and question them? Things change. Profoundly. What kind of a course could a person have done to prepare for being an "influencer"? That pursuit didn't exist ten years ago. Social media manager? Social media didn't exist back then either, so who could have imagined a job like that? Digital branding? Pop-up stores? A course in marketing, advertising, communications? Think about the useful skills that surround the field you are interested in.

Fashion editor at the *New York Times* Vanessa Friedman told me:

> One of the things that is so amazing about the world we live in now is that the jobs you think about now and the jobs you will probably be doing in ten years are completely different. The jobs you're bidding in ten years probably don't even exist now. People don't know what they're called, so it's very hard to kind of plan a career the way that people used to plan a career. Genres have become so fungible.

This may sound confusing, but it's also exciting. There are opportunities in places you may not have thought to look. Think about what's new, and then look at it closely and realize what its historical roots are. Think about its roots like Amanda Hesser did when she realized crowdsourcing was happening in the *New York Times* more than 160 years ago.

ZIGZAGS AND LEAPFROGS

A common myth is that you plan your career path from point A to B to C to D. In most cases, there isn't necessarily a linear path from point A to point D. Things happen. It's not usually a straight path. Most career paths zigzag and leapfrog. Unexpectedly. If you are prepared, you can take advantage of accidental opportunities and create a new path. That's what happened with Joy Reid.

Joy Reid on Zigzagging

I came out of Harvard with a degree in documentary film, which is very far away from being a premed. You can't do much with that degree, so I worked in various things, but my goal was really to be a storyteller, a writer and filmmaker. I did the next best thing. I got pregnant, and my husband and I moved to Florida. I wound up in local news.

I managed to last in local news until the Iraq War; I was very against it, so I ended up bailing out of news for a while. I worked on the 2004 campaign for an organization called America Coming Together, whose goal was to try to help John Kerry, but he was not really helpable as a political candidate. He lost. I then went into talk radio and started blogging and freelance writing. The first piece I sold was called "The Green Eggs and Jan," and it was a Dr. Seuss send-up about the Elián González story. I actually sold that. I realized I could make a hundred bucks writing. I was like, "This is great! I can be a writer. I have my own blog."

Talk radio was cool except that the people we were doing talk radio for decided to sell out of their talk stations a month before Barack Obama won the Iowa caucuses because they didn't think he had a shot. I wound up freelancing again, and the Obama campaign hired me because I had this mix of experience in news, writing, and radio. He won, which changes your prospects a lot in this business. My sort of weird jumble of experience happened to be exactly what you need to have to be a pundit because I knew a little bit about a lot of different things that all had to do with media and politics. I ended up doing a lot of punditry on MSNBC and CNBC.

I was a regular on Larry Kudlow's show on CNBC where it would be me against four conservatives, which was a great training ground for what I'm doing now. I ended up getting hired by NBC to run something called Grio, which was geared toward the African American community and experience. That got canceled. I became a reporter. Did a lot of Black Lives Matter stories and field stories. I did the Confederate flag coming down, and for the first time in my whole media career, I was a reporter. Then after Melissa Harris-Perry left her weekend show, they asked me to take over the hours, and the rest is history.

I spoke with Kathy Ireland about her transition from modeling to mogul. Considering her *Sports Illustrated Swimsuit Edition* success, she was premarketed in swimsuits. You would think her first venture into the fashion space would be swimwear, the proverbial "low-hanging fruit." She didn't. She started with socks.

Kathy Ireland
on Taking the Long View

When kathy ireland® Worldwide finally started, I was an aging, pregnant model at my kitchen table. There were some doors that were open because of my modeling career, but they were the wrong doors. They were doors of curiosity and ultimately doors that wasted each other's time. They weren't interested in my ideas as a CEO. I'm truly grateful that my modeling career ended up being my education and exposed me to the best designers in the world, travel, and people of all different cultures. But the job description was "Shut up and pose."

I was very specific about starting a brand and starting a company. I was looking at building something that would be lasting, not simply make a quick buck. I understood very early on in modeling how fickle people can be, and so I knew that it would have to be something with a real foundation. I also believed people wouldn't buy something just because it had my name on it. If this person is going to make the effort to shop, which is heroic, what are we contributing? I mean, today it's a little bit easier online, but even that takes an effort. The mother who's got kids in car seats and is just making it out of the driveway, that's a big deal. How are we going to serve her? How are we going to make her day better? And that journey began by asking a lot of questions.

Kathy took the classic entrepreneurial approach: She wanted to solve a problem. At the time, as a pregnant woman, she knew the day-to-day struggle it is for mothers to just go shopping. Her question was "How can I make her day better?"—which often meant making it easier. She did that and built a multibillion-dollar global business.

GETTING EXPERIENCE

There are many ways to gain an education, and building a creative career doesn't necessarily follow a linear line. Micaela Erlanger, who is the stylist for Lupita Nyong'o, Jared Leto, Meryl Streep, Common, Michelle Dockery, and many others, didn't even know the world of styling existed until she was exposed to it through a variety of internship programs and fieldwork.

Micaela Erlanger
on the Importance of Internships

I took a different internship every single semester, including summer and winter terms. You have to treat it like a job. I showed up early. I stayed late. You go above and beyond for the things that you're passionate about. I treated it like it was my priority and made myself invaluable. I wanted to soak up all of the experience and get all of the opportunity out of what was being offered to me. I looked at it as an opportunity to amass as much experience as I could so I had an understanding of what existed in our industry. When it came time to graduate, I had a better sense of the direction that I wanted to go in.

My senior year I landed an internship at Cosmopolitan *magazine. I fell in love with the work and thought I wanted to be a fashion editor. When I graduated, all the magazines were downsizing. The market sucked, but I had this internship and was able to extend it.*

Through that internship I met a celebrity stylist, Annabel Tollman, who was looking for an intern and hired me. She had been a fashion director at Interview *magazine and styled Jennifer Hudson, the Olsen twins, Mariah Carey, and Scarlett Johansson. I interned with Annabel for that year and then landed a position as an assistant costume designer on a New York Lottery commercial.*

That costume designer invited me to go to Los Angeles with her to work on a feature film, which is how I gave costume design a stint. I bought a one-way ticket and moved to LA. This is a real coming-of-age story. I had one suitcase with my blow-up mattress and styling kit and another suitcase with some clothes. I was the assistant costume designer on a low-budget Sundance film with Kate Mara, Octavia Spencer, and Taraji Henson before they were all superstars.

I finally had a sense of what this business was like. Costume design is very different, but I finally had credibility. I was getting paid for my work and building my portfolio. It was really valuable experience for me.

> *When I was back in New York, Annabel called and said, "You're doing great. I need a new assistant. Can I hire you?" I worked with Annabel five years longer. One day, the makeup artist from the second film called me and said, "I'm working with this actress. She's on this show called* Downton Abbey. *Her name is Michelle Dockery. She's nominated for a Golden Globe. She needs a stylist. Can I recommend you?" That was my first gig.*
>
> *At the end of our very successful Golden Globes and award-season run, Michelle said, "I have this friend. She's in a movie. You've never heard of her before. Her name is Lupita. She has a small film coming out. Can I recommend you?" Who knew that it was going to really launch my career? I think that that says something about being open to opportunity and exploring the world and exploring your field. Who knew that costume design would lead to Lupita Nyong'o, who won the Oscar that year?*
>
> *Annabel died very unexpectedly. Her family said, "We have this office with all this styling gear. What are we going to do with it?" They lived in London, and all of a sudden, I was being presented with an office lease and real responsibilities. I had to take this crazy freaking leap. I signed a commercial lease for seven years and emptied out my bank account. I started my business.*

Micaela's business has continued to grow, and she has become one of the most sought-after celebrity stylists. How she approached her internships was key to her success.

Most people wait to be told what to do. It's important to be proactive and figure the job out by paying attention and asking questions. Show your interest. Get your education. Make yourself important. It could become your next job.

New York Times investigative reporter Sarah Maslin Nir approached getting a job like she approaches her reporting: she got to know everybody and was willing to do anything.

I tell job seekers to report your way into a job. If you're an intern, you do not live nine to five. If you have the ability to get in a building, go to every other floor and talk to every single person there. I always say with a three-legged stool, make yourself that third leg because the thing can topple over without you. [The *New York Times*] ended up relying on me for tons of stuff. With no contract, I had my own nightlife column with the *New York Times*. I went to 252 parties in eighteen months.

I said to them, "I'm a little afraid to take this job because I have a fashion background, and I don't want to be seen as a blonde floozy." My editor said, "Reporting is reporting. If you can do one, you can do the other." Don't be dissuaded if you don't get the first job you want. Find out if there are ways that those skills are transferable. If you can go up to a celebrity on the red carpet and get something pithy out of them—something much more than "What are you wearing?"—you can do this.

Sarah's path led her to become a Pulitzer Prize–nominated journalist, a big change from going to 252 parties, but, interestingly, a lot of the same process. As she was told, "Reporting is reporting."

It's important to view a job beyond that one task. If you look at each job you get as the total worldview, it can kill your spirit. Part of being creative is overcoming obstacles. It's important to focus on what you want, not all the things in the way of it.

GETTING THE JOB

A mistake a lot of people make is applying for a job without a specific role in mind. They just want a job, so they are willing to do anything. The problem is, you can't expect the person on the other side of the desk to be your vocational guidance counselor.

You have to make their job easy by being specific about what job you are after. Designer Brandon Maxwell said:

> You're going for jobs, right? When you're out of school, you're like, what is a career now? People are getting a job, professionally doing Instagram. I have a sister who's twenty-one, and I'm like, "What are you going to do? You're graduating really soon." She's says, "I'm going to be a blogger." You have a hundred Instagram followers. What are you going to do with that? She says, "I'll get a camera. I'm going to be a blogger." I'm like, "Oh, my God, that's so awesome 'cause I'm running for president tomorrow."

The best way to look at internships is as a part of your curriculum. Look at it as a class to learn different aspects of a business you are interested in. If you are interested in fashion, intern at a public relations firm, a magazine, a clothing company, a retail store.

Whether you get a job or launch your own business, you will be starting from a much stronger knowledge base if you have that kind of experience.

Although focused on the fashion industry, Steven Kolb, CEO of the Council of Fashion Designers of America, has great advice that cuts across all careers:

> If you're interning or volunteering or have the opportunity to get involved with different parts of the industry, it's a good thing. I've seen people who've started careers in editorial cross over into fashion. Designers go into editorial. I think the more you know about the different categories of our industry, the better off you are. You're lucky you're in New York City. You have it all here. There are people who will contact us, and they'll be somewhere in the Midwest and want to work in fashion and how do they start? I always say get a job at J. Crew or the Gap or wherever because you can learn so much at retail.

SOME CAREERS ARE geographically centered in certain areas: Silicon Valley for tech, Los Angeles for film, New York for finance, fashion, and theater. That doesn't mean there aren't opportunities you can take advantage of in other locales and learn about what interests you.

It's also important to realize that an interview is a two-way communication. Go into an interview prepared. Ask questions. Display your knowledge of the company. It's not only about them wanting to hire you; it's also about learning if you want to work for them.

Another question that arises is what to do if you have a choice of either working for a large company, where you have a specific role, or working at a small company, where you have to do a lot of different things. I asked Dorie Clark what she thinks is a better choice.

The ideal choice is both, so over the course of your college and early career you can see what appeals to you more. If you have a strong preference for one or the other, honor that first. But if you're neutral about it, the best move would be to work for a large name-brand company.

The reason for that is a term that psychologists and sociologists use called "social proof." The basic idea is that you are going to get more respect and more credibility on your résumé and will be treated better by people because you have a name brand attached to you. This person has worked for Victoria's Secret; this person has worked for Nike. It's something that people have heard of, and you get the reflected glow of their brand on you. Even if later on you decide that you want to move to a smaller enterprise, you have the fact that you have been vetted by a famous corporation and they have deemed you worthy. It's an easier bar to clear when a smaller company is interviewing you because if you're good enough for Nike, you're probably good enough for them.

Victoria's Secret has been a client of mine for more than twenty years. They use a lot of interns. Over the years, they have hired interns from my class. Monica Mitro, executive vice president (EVP) of public relations, is a strong advocate of helping students gain experience:

> The number-one thing I recommend to you while you're in school is to get internships and start to work for people. I'm famous at Victoria's Secret for hiring interns, having them as my assistants, and then moving them up in the business. We've had interns go all the way up to vice president and move on to other companies. The best opportunity for us as companies is to hire interns and try them out.
>
> There's a woman who's been with me for about fifteen years. She called Victoria's Secret so many times, wanting to be an intern. I finally said to my team, "Just get her in here, and let's interview her." I would say the squeaky wheel does get the oil. I'm always really impressed by people who reach out and know what they want.

FOLLOWING UP AFTER an interview is essential. It demonstrates your interest in the position. The questions arise: How often should you follow up and how many times? Where is the line between being persistent and being a pain in the ass? Opinions are all over the place. There are no hard-and-fast rules, though there are a couple of simple and effective actions you can take to increase the possibility of getting a response. If you are following up after an interview at a place you'd like to work, hand-write a thank-you card and mail it to the person with whom you met. Emails are easy to ignore. These days it's a novelty to get an actual envelope with a handwritten response. It not only differentiates you but also shows that you are willing to take the time to reach out in a personal way. The other is to follow up with emails, and if you don't get a response after the second, put in the subject line, "I wanted to confirm you received my previous email." I have found people usually respond, but, at a certain point, a nonresponse is a response.

DO IT YOURSELF

Brandon Maxwell came into the public eye as Lady Gaga's fashion director. He started his much-acclaimed women's collection, enthusiastically welcomed by critics, and then the next season he was just as enthusiastically criticized by them. He learned the fickle nature of the fashion press and the perils of fame. He emerged wiser. He developed the confidence to follow his own direction. Fiercely. Brandon stopped listening to others. His business grew. He went on to win the coveted Council of Fashion Designers of America (CFDA) Award for "Womenswear Designer of the Year." I asked him about how he found his own voice and was able to follow it.

Brandon Maxwell
on Following His Own Voice

You're going to school to learn how to do something. Don't get it twisted when everybody's like, "You need to be the next." You don't need to be the next anybody; you only need to be you. That's it. Everybody's looking for the next something, and it's a joke.

Be yourself. Whatever you do is good enough, and do not start doing what people want. Throw a logo on it. Let's do a lower-price key chain. Forget a key chain. Who wants a key chain? That's not my market. That's not what I do. I'm not going to bend to do something else that everybody wants me to do because that's where the industry is going. Just sit on your horse and drive and stay strong. If you do weird work, whatever it is, do that, and somebody is going to come along and like it. Don't listen to everybody else. Take it from me. Write that down in your notebook. I've been through it. Don't pay attention to everybody, because nobody knows what they want.

You have to know what you're good at. Be confident. In creative careers, hard work really matters. Confidence is knowing that you might not be the best, you might not be the smartest, you might not be the most qualified, but you have what it takes inside to work hard to get there. That still matters.

It's a total roller coaster, and there is no assurance—ever. I wake up every day so unsure. Is my life over? Is my job over? But then I have to know that what I'm doing on some level eventually will matter. To somebody. And I get one message from a kid: "I'm so inspired by you." That's the best review I ever got. That's what it's all about, that one thing. Your brains and your minds matter. Use them wisely.

The work that you are making, the things that you are interested in, the things that you are doing do matter. Life and the arts are important. They're what we need more than anything. You have to have the confidence to know that. You will get knocked down so many times. All the people who have been successful and really made it, they're all the people who have been rejected. Have the courage to do it and have the confidence once you get there to just do your thing, live your life, whatever that is. If you're making a film, if you're an actor, a fashion designer, a hair stylist, makeup, do whatever. Don't let anybody tell you no. Do not go home after somebody tells you no and say, "Well, that's it for me." It's not. There are a lot of jobs out there.

Start your own thing. That's what I did. It's not easy. When no one would have me, I was like, I'll just do my own thing.

Max Vadukul knew he wanted to be a street photographer, which he felt expressed the true essence of photography: capturing a moment. He felt that if he could see the picture in the chaos, he would be a good photographer. Once his apprenticeship was over, I asked how he got to the next step.

Max Vadukul
on His Big Break

There was a famous film producer named David Puttnam. His was the agent for Guy Bourdin, Richard Avedon, and David Bailey in the sixties. I called his company, Enigma Productions, and left a message—"Please call Max Vadukul." That was it. Three months later, I'm watching wrestling on TV with my dad, and he says, "David Puttnam is on the phone."

I got straight to the point: "I'm a young photographer. I just want to show you my work. I'd like an opinion." He said, "I don't do that." There was silence for about six seconds, which was really a long time. He said, "Okay, I want to see six of your prints. If those six are any good, I'll call you."

He called me the next day. He laid them out on the floor, and he explained, "Max, you have a signature here. Don't change anything. Keep doing this. Don't stop."

I said, "But I need to make a living." He said, "Don't worry about the living. You're young. You can pick yourself up anytime you want. Don't listen to fashion people. Just do what you want. They will follow you." I said, "How do you mean?" He said, "They are only interested in finding the next trend, and then they claim it's theirs because they picked it up. You have to stick with what you have here. One day, you'll be a great photographer." As I was about to leave, he said, "I have a job for you. I want you to photograph four of my producers. I need portraits for public relations and the press."

I borrowed a camera and film from my brother. I gave David the contact sheets, and he said, "Where are you going? I need an invoice from you." I didn't know what an invoice was, and what he's basically doing is giving me a test. He's asking me to value myself, which I'd never done before. He's asking, "What are you worth?"

I sat down with my father and added up the bill. It came to six hundred pounds. I gave him the invoice. He looked at it and gave me a check on the spot. He said to me, "Six hundred pounds is a lot of money, Max. What are you going to do with it—party?" I said, "No, I'm going to take this and go to France and Italy, and I'm going to see if they love me there."

I took that check and got a flight to Paris. I was given three mag-azines that I had to see. At that time, it was French Elle, Marie Clare, and French Vogue. [One of the art directors] looks at the work, and he says, "You're totally wrong for us, but you're right for this guy. His name is Yohji Yamamoto. Go and see him."

I meet his legendary press guy, Marc Ascoli. Marc looks at the pictures and says, "Wait here." He brings out Yohji, who's this samurai-type guy. He's in all black and a very handsome guy.

He just goes, "Hi. You're going to shoot our next campaign. What do you want to do?" Just like that, I went from nothing—total rejection—to "You're going to shoot Yohji Yamamoto's next campaign."

Two days later we arrived in New York. I got paid because I demanded to be paid before I started. That wasn't because I'm a smart businessman or tough. I didn't have a camera. Imagine the risk I was taking. While they were doing hair and makeup, I took my cash and I went to Willoughby's. I bought a Nikon F3, a motor drive, and a bunch of film.

Today, the photos are still my written signature. That's how it started. We still work together.

DAYMOND JOHN HAD an idea, and that idea turned into FUBU. It took a few years for FUBU to get any traction, so it took a few years for him to give up his job at waiting tables. I asked about the challenges he faced starting out.

The first challenge was to get a group of people together who had the same agenda that I had, the same goals, and would not listen to all the people who told me that it couldn't be done.

The next challenge was understanding sourcing. My friend Jay was attending the Fashion Institute of Technology, and he would go and ask the professors, "Where do I get this fabric? Where do I do this?" There was no Internet. It was run around and try to find fabric or find this or find a seamstress.

The final issue was sales. How were we going to go out there and sell? There wasn't Twitter. There wasn't YouTube. If I sold you a shirt, I had to find you the next day and sell you another one. It was just all these challenges that we had, but, again, we were doing what we loved, and as I say to all the entrepreneurs, you have to take an affordable next step. People believe that you've got to go out there and have a $100,000 loan or $1 million loan. That's not going to make you any better. That's just going to make your debt larger.

That's what I did. We went out there, and we sold one, then we sold two, then we sold five, then we sold twenty.

A creative career, any career, every career, takes work. Developing a great work ethic is essential. It also is important to stay true to yourself and capitalize on your talents. Daymond worked hard on selling and marketing. You might think award-winning illustrator Yuko Shimizu spent her entire workday drawing. You'd be wrong.

One day a week, I just do paperwork, emailing and negotiating. I spend half of each day answering phone calls, replying to emails, or trying to think what the best way to write those emails when I say no to something because I don't want to come off as rude, or when I won't accept something because the fee is lower than I want.

My experience in the School of Visual Arts (SVA) was 90 percent of the time, we stayed in the studio. The life of the artist after school is half business, and it wasn't taught properly. I asked SVA to let me teach a class in business. It's not something I enjoy. I understand we came to art school to do art, so why the hell do I need to take business class? We made a short class, seven weeks. Each week we talk about different topics. Simple things, like you should get your own email address; your name at your domain dot-com because it looks professional. If you're in group mail with multiple artists, most of them are name at

Gmail.com; you can find them, but it's extra work. If you have the domain, it looks professional.

If you're pitching for a job, you're negotiating terms and fees. How you write an email and how you come off to them might help. In art school, you don't really learn those things. I felt those things are very important.

It makes perfect sense to have your own domain name as opposed to Gmail. That's great, simple, and cheap advice. You can still use your name for Gmail with your friends. This also helps you keep your personal and business emails separate.

Here are some tips for responding effectively and professionally via email: Be polite. Write something that indicates you have done your homework. You can say you like someone's work or congratulate them on something you read. Do some research on the person or the company. Ask questions, but only ask questions you actually care about. Don't just go through the motions, as people can sense that. If you read some interviews and said, "I read the article about you and was curious about X," if something is written well and demonstrates that you did your homework, you will usually get a response before someone who didn't.

The same principles apply to interviews. Do your homework, know who you are talking to, and err on the side of being more polite and formal than casual until you get the vibe from the person that you can be that way. It's about building relationships, and your most primary relationship is with yourself. Finding your own voice is essential in any creative pursuit. That's your distinguishing difference. That's also a challenge. Knowing who you are and having the confidence to not only express that but also have the persistence to deal with the criticism are essential. As Brandon Maxwell said, "It's a roller-coaster ride."

Workbook Questions

- What valuable lessons have your learned from previous career setbacks, and how can you apply them to your goals?

- What do you want to do that you haven't done?

- How can you fill the holes in your knowledge with hands-on experience?

- What are the criteria for writing an effective email?

- What questions would you want to ask at an interview?

5

Assessing Risk

I TOOK A RISK WRITING this book. A book is a big commitment of time and effort with potentially little financial reward because there is no guarantee it will be bought. (I hope you paid for the copy you are reading.) If my goal is to share what I think are valuable ideas that can help people think about their career in a meaningful way, I have no guarantee that it will be read. Writing a book, especially by an unknown first-time author, is like yelling at a cloud of smoke.

You are taking a risk reading it. You might not think it was worth your time or your money. Your risk is less. You can stop reading it. Sell it. Give it away. There are differences in degree of risk. Millions of people risk a few dollars a week on hopes of winning millions of dollars on the lottery. You have a 1 in 22,528,737 chance of winning. In all aspects of risk, the common thread is not knowing with certainty what the outcome is going to be.

The important question around risk is how to assess and get comfortable with it so that you can push your creative boundaries beyond what is safe, predictable, and boring.

Debbie Millman, a graphic designer, author, brand consultant, and the host of the award-winning podcast *Design Matters*, says that you can't achieve anything remarkable without risking your own comfort or your reputation. While many people believe that they need only confidence to become comfortable taking risks, Debbie says it's about courage, not confidence. She defines confidence as the successful repetition of an endeavor. Courage, on the other hand, is taking the first step off the cliff before you have a chance to build up confidence.

What Does Risk Mean to You?

I define risk as calculating how much you're willing to fail. We all have a different tolerance for failure. Some of us are able to pick ourselves off the floor a hundred times before we find that great idea. Some of us have no tolerance for that. When you think about taking a risk, it's "How willing to fail am I today?"

—RANDI ZUCKERBERG

I don't understand the concept of risk, which is good for me. If you're going to do stuff and you're thinking about all the risks associated with it, you could convince yourself not to do anything. There's always a better time to wait to do something. If Steve Jobs thought about the risk, we wouldn't have the iPhone. To anyone pioneering anything, risk is a nonexistent word to them.

—RYAN URBAN, CEO AND FOUNDER OF BOUNCEX

I define risk as seeing opportunity and not being afraid to take it. Risk is good for you. It's good vitamins.

—JOY-ANN REID

I think that everything we do is a risk. I think every effort that I've put out, half or less than half are going to be successful. That's when I am fully confident. I think risk is when I have little information, but I'm going to take a gamble on it.

—DAYMOND JOHN

> *Risk is the opposite of learning. Once you learn something, risk becomes smaller.*
>
> **—MORAN CERF**
>
> *Risk to me is the probability of an irreversible negative outcome. I've thought about this a lot because I think there's a huge misconception that entrepreneurs are these huge risk takers.*
>
> *Is that the reality for most of the extremely successful entrepreneurs I've met? Not at all. They are very good at assessing what is reversible and what is not, what is temporary and what is permanent, and they are good at placing small bets. That's it.*
>
> **—TIM FERRISS**

PUSHING BOUNDARIES

Think of risk on a scale of one to ten. One represents almost no risk, whereas ten is catastrophic and life changing. Free climbing is a ten. Risking all your savings on a lottery ticket is a ten. Most things are a two, three, or four; they aren't that big a risk when you carefully evaluate them.

Look at what's scaring you, because the more frightened you are, the more you perceive something as risky. It is important to ask yourself, "What am I really afraid of? Am I afraid of not knowing the outcome? Being embarrassed? Getting rejected? Failing? Losing money? Physical harm?" Looked at with some context and perspective, most things don't involve that much risk. What is the worst-case scenario? If you're jeopardizing your family, your home, your livelihood, your health, that requires significant risk assessment.

Taking a risk is not always a calculated decision. Events in our lives that we could have never expected change the landscape of our decisions, and we are willing to take risks that we might not have taken before. I spoke with artist Zaria Forman about how unforeseen circumstances changed her life.

Zaria Forman
on Going Outside Her Comfort Zone

One of the most valuable lessons I've learned is to take risks. The first, biggest risk I took with my work was leading an expedition to Greenland. I traveled often with my family growing up for my mother's fine-art photography, but I never had to plan the trips myself and never thought I would be capable of doing so.

We were planning a trip together to go to Greenland and mirror an expedition that had happened in 1869, led by an American painter, William Bradford. It was the first Arctic expedition where the main purpose was art, as opposed to science or exploration. My mom thought it would be fascinating to travel up the northwest coast of Greenland, follow their path, and be inspired by the same landscape almost 150 years after they had.

We were in the early stages of planning this trip when my mother was diagnosed with brain cancer, and she passed away six months later. Her dedication to the expedition, though, never wavered, and I made a promise to carry out her final journey, which I did in August 2012, leading a group of scholars and artists on a four-week expedition. The undertaking was terrifying at first. I didn't want to do it, but I felt like it was my duty. Persevering through that terror, and accomplishing what I set out to do, made me realize that I could actually do it! It may be the biggest gift that my mother gave me because it made me recognize that I was actually capable of undertakings that I didn't think I was.

Every time I push my boundaries and do something that feels terrifying and I'm not sure if I'll succeed, I learn the most and grow the most in my career. Even if it's not as "successful" as I hoped it would be, I still learned so much from the experience, which I think makes it successful. It's not about the end goal. It's about going through something, a process that feels uncomfortable, where you're not sure what you're doing and you're learning as you go. If you don't push your personal boundaries and try something outside your comfort zone, you won't grow as an artist.

When one refers to entrepreneurs, they are most often talking about someone who starts a business. Artists, actors, musicians, and performers are true entrepreneurs—maybe the truest, because there is no proof of concept until they succeed. They are constantly at risk because they are the product. There is no business plan to follow. There is no problem they are solving or need they are fulfilling in the traditional product/service model. Zaria's entrepreneurial mind-set not only set her on the journey she had hoped to go on with her mother but was also the foundation of her career as an artist.

Our relationship with and perception of risk are major factors when making dramatic life decisions. Leaving a job is such a decision. So is relocating. Changing careers is an even bigger risk. When Yuko Shimizu made the decision to leave her job where she had a steady paycheck and benefits, she did all three at once. I asked her how she assessed the risk. How did she make the decision to not only to leave her job but move and change careers as well?

> I don't like regret. The worst regret is, you know something you should be doing and you have not done it. If you have done it and it didn't work out, you worked hard and it didn't work out, but you can move on because you tried. I always wanted to go to art school and never did. I met someone who had graduated from art school, and I didn't know how to speak to them because I felt like I was inferior. That person did something I wanted to do and had never done. That feeling never went away. Every time I meet someone who went to art school, I felt self-conscious. That went on for more than ten years. I didn't want to get old and say, "I wish I would have done that."

Most of us have had the feeling of "I could've done that," whether at an art gallery, watching a performance, or finding a new product or even a new business idea. What's the difference between you and them? They actually did it. You didn't.

A lot of people have good ideas, but risk stops those without an entrepreneurial mind-set from actually doing them. Neuroscientist and professor Moran Cerf says that entrepreneurs have a specific mind-set that is not paralyzed by risk.

Moran Cerf on Baby Steps

It's a mind-set that is more tolerant of risk and that is in love with an idea to the point where they're willing to sacrifice a lot for their goal. Those two components are enough to chase something that on paper makes no sense. You sometimes find people telling you that it's a bad idea and it's risky. Humans hate risk and bad feedback.

An entrepreneur is a person who overcomes this. You create a mind-set by saying, "I don't care. I'm going to see the light at the end of the tunnel despite all the things that the immediate world suggests are not good."

In the brain, we have a mechanism that defines risk for us. We can look at it in a very clinical way, but from our perspective, it's usually lack of knowledge.

I spent time talking to people working at the circus. There are people who walk on a tightrope twenty feet aboveground, and if you not only see them but also measure their body, you'll see that they actually don't experience risk in the sense that there's no elevation in the heart rate; they don't sweat like we do.

If you ask them, "Are you not feeling risk?" they say something like, "The first time I felt it, but over time I know more, and now I just do it. It doesn't feel like risk because I have full control."

It's the same way when you go down the stairs: you don't feel risk, and you just walk down the stairs. When you were a baby, you felt risk. You walked up to them—this was a risky moment—and you actually had to move. Somehow across life, you learned it and it became a mechanical operation that you know how to do without feeling risk.

If you fall and you break something, you will go back to the beginning; you will feel risk again. Your brain is made to save your life when in the face of danger. So when danger comes, you will actually go back to the process.

Once you learn something, risk becomes smaller. So you are less afraid of being in class than you were on the first day you came here. You're less afraid to speak up than you were a few years ago. You will be less afraid on your second company than you will be on the first time when you raise money for a seed company. The more you learn or experience, the risk becomes smaller in any domain, good or bad.

The restaurant business is extremely risky. There are twenty thousand restaurants in New York City. As chef and co-owner of Vic's, Hillary Sterling says she has to prove herself every day and convince her customer to come back every time.

I asked Hillary how she assesses risk and determines which ones are worth taking. In every creative field, there are designers, artists, and chefs who are faulted for doing the same thing they always did. Of course, there's the market that will buy the same thing they always did, but when it's so competitive you have to give people a reason to buy, you need to give people a reason to come back and eat at your restaurant, so they need to know they're not only going to get a great meal but sometimes be surprised by something new.

A friend of mine took a new job that is going to be in the spotlight. I looked at his menu; it was food we did together nine years ago. He's doing food he knows how to make and he knows is delicious. Only a handful of us know that he's taking a shortcut. I want to support him. I'll go eat that food that we did nine years ago. I was really disappointed when I read the menu, but I also understand where he's coming from.

When you are in the spotlight and people are judging you every minute of the day, and if you fail, you'll be fired, or your restaurant goes out of business, it's not just a failure—it's a multimillion-dollar failure. No restaurant opens up in New York City anymore for under $2 million, so if you fail, it is $2 million gone. Who's paying that back? We happen to be three and a half years old, so safe is about consistency now and making sure I greet those guests and make it personal. For him, safe is being alive in six months.

A FEW YEARS ago, my wife and I went to see James Taylor at a sold-out performance at Madison Square Garden. Partway through the concert, after singing "Carolina on My Mind," James announced he was going to sing some of his new songs. There was a groan from the audience. He said, with tongue in cheek, "Don't worry. My new stuff sounds just like my old stuff." It depressed me. He became popular by having a unique sound, by doing something different. It was his fans who put him in the golden handcuffs, instead of realizing the reason they liked him in the first place was because he was different.

Playing it safe can be a risk, too. At a certain point, if you aren't offering anything new, your audience has no reason to buy. They already heard it, have something like it, have no reason to purchase it. It's about achieving the right balance: offering something new so there is a reason to come back, while maintaining the things that brought people in the first place. Even McDonald's varied their menu to stay competitive. Ralph Lauren can continue selling his polo shirts season after season, year after year, while people look at and buy his newer offerings. It's true in every business.

HOW TO CALCULATE RISK

Whatever you are selling, achieving the right balance of new along with what you know your audience wants is a tightrope walk.

As part of Strategic Coach, Dan Sullivan counsels high–net worth business owners on how to assess risk. Risk is an ongoing concern for entrepreneurs. Dan applies an interesting time-traveling technique for assessing risk.

Dan Sullivan on
Trying to Look into the Future

You can never assess risk in the present. Whatever you are thinking about doing is possibly a risk. Imagine yourself three years in the future. Three years is a phenomenally good time frame, and the reason is that we can actually imagine it. It's the year after the year after next. Most people can visualize that. You get out five years, ten years, and most people can't. Next year is a little bit too soon.

Run two paths out to three years in the future. The first one is you are going to make the decision to do the new activity. How are you three years from now as a result of having done this? Best-possible circumstances? Then imagine not doing that and not doing anything else for the next three years but being where you are. How are you if you haven't taken on this new activity three years from now? Ask yourself, which is the better three years?

You can only assess risk against a future outcome, and that's a skill. A lot of people don't have this skill. It's like going to the gym: The more you do it, the more this visualization of the future actually increases. If you are going to do this, then what during the next ninety days do you have to do so that three-year thing actually happens? That's where the strategic game plan really starts.

Essentially, what the person has done is that they have created a future self, and a future self can't take action; only the present self can take action, but the future self can talk to the present self. I'm operating right now because I've been at this a long time with a very good idea of who Dan Sullivan is going to be when he is ninety-five years old, physically, mentally, financially, what my relationships are going to be like, and what my self-assessment will be when I'm twenty-five years older. That person talks to me. For example, when I get up, do I feel like exercising? I said, "Well, what would your ninety-five-year-old self say about whether you should exercise? Get down there and start exercising!" I have this time frame, and I'm in a zone now because above seventy most people are starting to check out and I'm not checking out. I've got to pay attention to this future self.

I try to train all the entrepreneurs in the program to keep developing this future self who gives them this very good direction about what they ought to be doing right now. Within the framework of that, there are a lot of risks that they are going to have to take. You're going to have to change things, eliminate things, and add things. You're going to have to take financial risks and time risks. That's really what it's all about.

Stephanie Jones is the founder and CEO of JONESWORKS, a full-service, strategy-driven public relations, marketing, and communications agency. Prior to starting her company, she worked at a multibillion-dollar advertising agency, Deutsch, Inc., where she served as vice president. After establishing herself as a successful VP, Stephanie left to start her own company and pursue her passion in PR, marketing, and communications. I asked her how she assessed the risk, overcame the doubt, and made the leap into the unknown.

In the beginning, I paid myself a small salary and paid the people who were working with me more, so I could recruit them. It was scary issuing my first big payroll, purchasing laptops, and managing travel expenses. I was stepping out of my comfort zone and pitching potential clients with no guarantee we'd win their businesses. I worked with clients like Kendra Scott, who started with $500 selling jewelry door-to-door with her baby. Her brand would later become valued at over $1 billion.

You have to start small, you have to scale strategically, and you have to do what you know is vital. Don't try to take on too much. Some of the most important things are what we say no to because it means we're saying yes to only a few select things.

Starting a business is easy. Building and sustaining it is hard. Based on Harvard Business School research, the failure rate of all US companies after two years is 40 percent, over 50 percent in five years, and over 70 percent after ten years. Although the odds are not great, you can improve your chances of success by employing smart business practices, whether you are running a big business or an artist, knowing your costs and margins are important for survival. Oliver Jeffers does just that:

With my books, I've learned to try and be as economical as possible in terms of both style and color, 'cause that just will lead to the simplicity of reproduction. So I tend to use colored pencil, gouache watercolor, slightly more in the books, things that reproduce easier.

Oil paint is very tricky to reproduce in an accurate way, so I tend to keep oils exclusively for one-off paintings. Whenever you work at a massive scale and then reduce it down to fit in a book, oftentimes it loses something in translation. All the art that I make for books tends to be made at exactly the size that the book is so that there's no massive shift in the weight of the line from the original to reproduced form. It's always there at the back of your head, even if you're just making art that's purely for self-expression. There are practicalities involved in that the whole way along. So when you're doing the books and you know these colors reproduce easier, I can get this done and this will create less problems. If you want to be successful, you have to be aware of how much it costs to actually manufacture what it is, without question.

Whether it is a painting, clothing, a computer, or a television series, the costs of material and labor time are factors that need to be considered.

Josh Sapan is the CEO of AMC Networks, a $3 billion publicly traded company. I will always love AMC for green-lighting *Mad Men* and *Breaking Bad*. All decisions involve risk and have to be evaluated thoroughly because the consequences can be enormous for the company and its stockholders. I asked Josh how they evaluate risk when deciding whether to commit to a new program. What kind of data is the most useful when making decisions?

It cuts to a lot of where decision making is made. It's the era of big data. We all read about that, and it's true. There's a lot of information kicking around, and we are figuring out how to manage it and make it useful. Before a show premieres, we get awareness information about how many people have heard of it, so we know before it premieres whether our marketing is working.

We do focus groups, conventionally on pilots, and see how they like them. We do this thing called ASI testing where you watch a TV show with dials in your hands, and when you like it, you go like that [turns the dial to the right]. When you don't, you go like that [turns the dial to the left]. You could also get yourself so confused you won't know what day it is if you use much of this stuff because you can get faked out.

The data I find the most interesting is when you get Nielsen data. You get what's called minute-by-minute. When a show goes on, you can see it go like this [up, then down]. Oftentimes, unfortunately, it takes your breath away, which means you got a lot of people to watch and they tuned out during the show, which means that you get them there, but they weren't liking it too much.

I find it interesting that in spite of there being a lot of really smart people, a lot of computers, a lot of data, focus groups, and so on, there are so many failures. I asked Josh to explain that. He said, "That is a pleasurable answer: the intangible qualities that make something appealing on the screen are not entirely diagnosable, and there's 'the magic thing.'"

All businesses look at risk and try to minimize it. However, there are movies and shows that test great—and bomb. There are shows that don't test well and are huge successes. Every network turned down *Mad Men*. AMC was trying to make the transition from a movie channel (AMC stands for "American Movie Classics") to a network like HBO. HBO had great success with *The Sopranos*. That was proof of concept for an edgy, continuing dramatic series. AMC green-lit *Mad Men* because the idea of the show reminded the person in charge of the world he grew up in, watching his father, who was in advertising on Madison Avenue. He knew how rich the territory was for a continuing drama. That person in charge was Josh Sapan. He saw "the magic thing" in the show and was willing to risk it. In this case, "the magic thing" was intuition.

IBM could have owned the personal computer business, but the testing they did concluded that men would not want a keyboard on their desk, as it would make them feel like secretaries. IBM made its fortunes on gigantic mainframe computers and didn't see the market for personal computers. The risk wasn't worth it. Apple thought different.

When Ron Chernow, the National Book Award–winning author, was approached by Lin-Manuel Miranda to work on a hip hop musical with a mixed-race cast playing the founding fathers, he was intrigued by the idea. "My friends thought I was crazy, that it would never work." The risk paid off. *Hamilton*, based on Chernow's biography of Alexander Hamilton, went on to become one of the biggest hits in Broadway history.

When you're dealing with something as fickle as the public's taste, it's difficult to pinpoint what's going to be successful and what isn't. Betting on your success is a risk. The question is whether you are willing to bet on yourself.

WHEN TO GO ALL IN

When does your side hustle become the hustle? When do you give up your job and devote all your time and energy into making your business happen?

"Follow your passion" is wonderful-sounding advice until you realize your passion may have an impact on others: your partner, children, parents, and employees. There is a lot to think about before you take that leap. How do you determine when to go all in?

Daniel Gulati is a managing director for Comcast Ventures, an early-stage investment capital firm. His charge is to find companies that he thinks are a good investment. He has met with many entrepreneurs on the threshold of "going all in."

I asked Daniel when he thought one should make the leap from their day job to devoting all their time to their new company.

Starting a company from scratch is a highly irrational act. For the vast majority of people reading this, keeping a steady day job and predictable career path will be the superior economic option.

Therefore, to jump ship and start a company, you have to pass at least one of two tests. The first test is you are in that small minority of people whose expected value of starting a company exceeds the expected value of keeping their current job. The second is you have strong nonfinancial motivations behind starting a company. This is typically an obsession with a particular problem you are trying to solve or the desire for autonomy and decision-making power.

As an early-stage venture capital investor, my goal is to invest in talented entrepreneurs who are capable of building companies that make a significant impact in the world. The flip side is an acknowledgment that starting these types of companies from scratch is incredibly difficult, and most people who attempt to do so will fail. To use a baseball analogy, a VC's focus is less on batting average and more on the number of home runs we hit.

Given that VC is a power-law business, I am focused on partnering with entrepreneurs with big visions for how the world can be better and who have the capabilities to pull off something extraordinary. Typically, these business ideas have a contrarian feel to them—if everyone agreed, there wouldn't be an opening for a tiny start-up. So rather than assessing risk, I am interested in understanding what happens when the entrepreneur's hunch turns out to be correct.

I had a hunch that there was a market for the kind of clothing I would want to wear. I sketched some designs and had the people who did alterations for the store make the clothes. They sold out immediately. We made more. They sold out just as fast. I packed some samples into a suitcase, strapped it onto the back of my Triumph motorcycle, and drove to Chicago. I went to eighteen boutiques and sold to fourteen of them. I had my proof of concept—$135,000 in orders—but I had no idea how I would get the clothing made. My double major, philosophy and psychology, combined with being on the wrestling team, was the perfect combination for entering the world of business.

Daymond John had proof of concept, and that created a problem. At the Magic Show in Las Vegas, Daymond's company, FUBU, wrote more than $300,000 in orders. He had no money and had maxed out his credit cards getting to Vegas. Now he had to finance the orders. First, he had to find the money to produce what he sold.

I went to Vegas with an empty suitcase because I thought they were going to give me the cash there. I'm not lying. When it hit me that I had to make $300,000 worth of clothes, I tried to get a banker. I came home to my mother and said, "I got turned down by twenty-seven banks." She said, "I didn't even know twenty-seven banks existed." She said, "Okay, if you have $300,000 in orders, I want to take a second equity mortgage on the house." We took that for $100,000 because we owned our house outright. We kept paying it down. She said, "When you sell the $300,000 worth of product, you put the $100,000 back."

Daymond was at an interesting juncture. FUBU was starting to take off, but his only secure income was his job at Red Lobster. When do you make the jump? How do you determine when you're going to go all in?

We're at $300,000 to $500,000 where you say, "Wait a minute. The business is calling me more than my day job." Then you have the $2 million to $3 million mark where it's "All right, we've been doing this for quite some time. We may be a little bit in the red or in the black, but we've built this thing. Do we try now to become a real brand? Get venture in or a strategic partner?"

My business started calling me around $50,000 to $75,000, when I felt that, "If I went and put my time in there, I could take the business up to $150,000 and I can pull out $30,000 to live." At that point, that's what I did.

Designer Brandon Maxwell took a different approach. He wanted to start a company that catered to high-end fashionable women. He saved every paycheck until he had what he thought was enough money to start his business and dove right in. He grossly underestimated what it would take.

That money went in less than a month. Then you've done a show that you have not planned to go anywhere that's now being bought in stores, written about everywhere, and winning awards. Nightmare.

I had no idea how to produce clothes, no team to produce the clothes, no money to keep the lights on, and everybody's watching you. It was terrifying. I thankfully had my dad, who is a well-known businessman, who jumped in and helped me. I did every job I could to pay the bills. I worked collection one day, another job the next day, collection one day, now another job, until I was exhausted. I was on an airplane ten times a week, just trying to keep the lights on. It's a vicious cycle. You can't stop because you're so grateful to be there. It's not the way that you thought it was going to be, and the pressure is so much. Then I'm doing all these interviews and tired and stressed all the time and trying to build a team. I had no idea of any of that.

I went into the real world and realized that there's nothing quite like the feeling of waking up in the morning and feeling like you're hanging out over a ledge in front of everybody and you're going to fall and you're going to be out of money and people are still going to know you. "What happened to him?" That really messes with your mind. And then at the same time that's happening, the collection is due like last week. "Are we making any progress on that?"

Every day I had to wake up and decide I'm going to make it through this because people go through this. People try to run you through the gauntlet, and that's what this career is about: shooting you up to watch your fall just to see how you can handle it. And what I realized after the first year is that they do that on purpose to see if you have the courage and confidence to keep going. I had to wake up every day and be like, "Yeah, I'm going to do this today." You have to do that, too.

Some entrepreneurs advise caution. When she was first starting out, award-winning illustrator Yuko Shimizu was strategic about taking affordable next steps. She budgeted how much money she needed to live and how many illustrations she needed to sell in order to make ends meet. Then she went all in on pursuing her dream knowing exactly what she needed to do to earn a living doing illustration.

When I graduated, I went to talk to one of my professors who had his own design studio. I was really worried. Should I get a day job? What should I do? He asked me how much I needed to pay all my bills. It was 2003. I was in Greenpoint [Brooklyn]. I had two roommates. We didn't even have high-speed Internet in the area. It was a twenty-minute walk to the train station, so the rent was pretty cheap. We had a very cheap supermarket nearby.

If I had $2,000, I could pay all my bills, and you have to pay tax, too, so you need $2,500 to live. I did have small amount of money left in my bank account. If I lived on $2,000 a month for everything, then I can live for maybe five, six months. My professor said, "Okay, average spot illustration pays about $500. You need $2,500 to pay tax and pay all your bills. If you get five jobs a month, you can pay everything. If you get a starting full-time job, you probably will get the same amount of money, but you won't have a lot of time to build your portfolio to sell your work to clients."

You don't have to think of getting a day job right now. Focus on spending your free time making new work, build your portfolio, and put it on your website. Send a promotional card, make cold calls, call magazines, and ask for a portfolio drop-off date. Try to get five jobs. In the beginning it's hard, but the more work you do, the more your artwork gets circulated.

Understanding your overhead is extremely important. "I'd like to have the $4.75 Starbucks, but I'll have the 65-cent deli coffee instead." Those kinds of decisions may be necessary when you're starting out, if you don't have the funding and if you're making it on your own. Your life is a business; you have overhead. You've got your expenses for your rent, cell phone, food, transportation, dental bills, and clothes, et cetera. You have to calculate, just like any other business.

You want to make sure that you don't go too far into debt. If you get that fallback job or that day job, you also have to think about how much time you're sacrificing that you could be putting toward the work you actually want to do. Calculate your budget. It's not easy to get those jobs initially. But it's a lot harder and longer process if you get a day job and, at the same time, try to get the work you want to do.

The question of when to make that leap from your corporate job to your start-up is a very personal one and requires an assessment of your status: income level, risk tolerance, potential impact if you have a family. Dave Asprey had a good career in Silicon Valley. However, he had a bigger goal for himself: go all in and build the Bulletproof brand. The biggest deciding factor for Dave was internal.

There's a feeling in your chest. If you meditate or you have some spiritual practice, you can feel there's a fear and there's an excitement down in the gut. Something happens when you realize that the excitement's bigger than the fear, and that's when you should do it. You want to be a bit practical about it and look at the bank account. Can you make ends meet? Look at who's counting on you. If you're single, you can move to Bali and do it; you can go to all sorts of places. You have so much flexibility. You may have a six-month runaway and you're good to go, or you have a twelve-month runaway if you go somewhere cheaper. It's either going to work or not going to work. If you're doing this when you're older . . . I started full-time at forty-one, which means I have two kids, I have a house payment, cars, and infrastructure, and it also means I'm not going to disappear off to some third world country and live on a beach because I have responsibilities. The bottom line is I have to make this much every month or my family isn't safe. You need to know what that number is.

Dan Sullivan points out one of the major stumbling blocks most entrepreneurs have to deal with:

> You get the job, and then you have to be fully at the job to fulfill the contract. You don't have time for marketing and sales to make sure that there's going to be future cash flow. It takes a while to get the rhythm where you have to be doing both of them at the same time.
>
> To be an entrepreneur, there's confidence, but there's also a fair amount of ignorance. The ignorance is a very important strength because if you really knew the true risks that you were taking, you would probably not do it.
>
> A lot of people's self-identity and their sense of worth as an individual come from being employed and being part of someone else's structure. The entrepreneur has to supply that sense of status and self-worth on their own. That's actually the first creation that the entrepreneur ever does before creating something to sell.

Oliver Jeffers reinforces this:

> It comes down to just how much you value what it is that you have to say and how you ranked that with financial security. At that point, I didn't have kids. I had a small studio, but I could either have really nice stuff and really nice vacations or I could be making the art that I want to make. It's like jumping into a swimming pool. You go down before you come back up. It's a risk that I never doubted for a second. I've never looked back.

A LOT OF people want to start their own business. Figuring out how to make your business work is a survival skill. If there are other people who are in the same business doing well and you're not, there's nothing wrong with the business you're in—there's something wrong with you. If you go into another industry, you're going to spend another year learning the technical skills so you can go out and repeat the same bad business habits that have caused you to be failing in what you're doing now. It's important to learn fundamental business skills.

Until you learn fundamental business principles, you'll spend your life pursuing opportunities, when what you need to do is learn how to make a business work. The same principles apply to whatever business you are in.

You have to put yourself at risk, make the leap, and bet on yourself. Go all in, whether you are starting a job or a business— but educate yourself first. There are a lot of resources available. Read, research, go to a conference, and meet people with similar goals and interests. Figure out how to make your business work. Never stop selling. Never stop learning.

Breaking down the time, the labor, the materials is just like designing clothes. It's just like being an architect. A filmmaker. An artist. It's just like every other kind of work. Being an artist requires a certain skill set. But the protocols about making a living at it are the same no matter what it is you decide to do. And it's important to understand that because so many people put up these different barriers between the disciplines, and they don't really exist. If you want to make a living as an artist, then you have to know these things. If you want to make a living as a bricklayer, you've got to know these things. Yeah. It's all kind of the same. The difference is how you value what you do.

....

Workbook Questions

💡 Whose sense of risk do you relate to and why?

💡 How do you define risk?

💡 What are your priorities right now? How important is structure, a sense of security, steady income?

💡 Can you tolerate not knowing what the future holds? Be flexible? Live without income for a period of time?

💡 What is an affordable next step you can take toward pursuing your creative career?

💡 Once you figure out what labor and materials are needed and cost it out, can you sell the end product at a profit?

💡 Can you make enough money to pay your bills if you go all in?

💡 How can you keep a steady sales effort going when you are busy?

....

6

Overcoming Fear and Doubt

WE EXPERIENCE FEAR AND DOUBT for evolutionary reasons. They are survival responses. There was a good reason to take this path rather than that path, because that path led you to danger: predatory animals, opposing tribes, or impassable terrain. People are afraid of the dark for the simple reason that they can't see what's out there. Fear is visceral; we feel it, rational or not. Doubt is intellectual. You have to think about something in order to doubt it.

Creativity, by definition, involves doing something unfamiliar, and as a result it can cause fear and doubt. When you put yourself out there, you risk rejection, criticism, and unknown outcomes, none of which feel good. Going beyond the borders means going into unchartered territory. "Think outside the box" has become so common that the phrase itself is inside the box.

Fear and doubt are inexorably tied to risk. If there is no fear, there's no risk—at least not one you perceive. Doubt is questioning your ability to control an outcome. Risk is assessing the potential gain against potential loss. What they have in common is that they can stop you.

As Elie Wiesel said, the opposite of love is not hate but indifference. That's the most painful thing. You can deal with somebody loving you. You can even deal with somebody hating you.

Indifference is really difficult to deal with because then the relationship is over. To be distinctive, you need to stand for something. Not everybody is going to like what you do. Some people might love it; some people will hate it. A creative person hates indifference. It is important to realize what our emotional triggers are and what really affects us. We shouldn't be afraid of hatred; we should deal with it. We shouldn't be afraid of love; we should deal with it. Indifference? My approach is to confront it and try to understand it. Unless I'm indifferent to your indifference, I'm going to get you on one side or the other. Indifference is lack of engagement, and lack of engagement is the worst thing for a creative person.

CONFRONT YOUR FEARS

Most of us develop a fear of rejection at an early age that makes us risk averse and quashes our natural creativity and makes us afraid to express ourselves. If you go along with the status quo and don't make waves, it's easy to avoid taking risks. It starts young. Remember the feeling you had the first day of class? The first day on a job?

A common, sometimes paralyzing fear is speaking in front of others. You wouldn't know it if you met him now, but Joe Polish grew up being very introverted. A big part of what he does is speak in front of crowds. He does it extremely well, but that didn't come easy.

The first time I ever did a speech, I was scared shitless. I wrote a sales letter for a seminar that I was doing in 1994 for carpet cleaners. I got fifty-two people to sign up for ninety-seven dollars a person. It was an all-day event with me speaking all day. People would tell me, "After the first two or three minutes of talking, you know, the nervousness will subside, and you'll be okay." The entire day I was just a nervous wreck. I was sweating. I literally used to get sick when I spoke in the very beginning, because I was so shy and nervous about doing it. But I did it.

What I learned is that which you fear and don't face controls you. That which you fear, and you take steps to face, you can control or at least get better at dealing with.

I also learned that I'm never going to get anywhere in my life if I don't interact with other human beings. So I forced myself. I'm an extroverted introvert. I literally go out and just do it. I had to go through a long period of time to just get used to it. Then I realized, "No one is going to hurt me by talking to them." You can learn anything if you do it enough.

There are some creative ways to help you overcome the fear of speaking in front of a group. Taking an improv acting or comedy class is a terrific way to learn how to interact with people, even though the idea of it will scare you at first. It's actually fun.

How can you overcome your fear and stop letting it get in the way of your creativity? Confront it. If you are afraid to decide, decide anyway. Again. And again. You will realize it didn't kill you. The more you get used to something, the more you can deal with it. Speaking in front of others might never be fun for you—it might always be something you don't like—but after you've done it a few times and allowed yourself to realize your world didn't end as a result of speaking up, you will be less afraid and more able to do it. It requires the courage to move out of what's comfortable for you, which is necessary to pursue any creative career.

Behavioral scientist Jon Levy spoke to me about doubt:

I have lots of doubts. It's important to have doubts. Anybody that has absolutely certainty in something, probably has a high chance of being wrong. Adam Grant did a study asking, "Is it important to be an arrogant leader, to say 'Yes, we can accomplish these goals,' or is it important to be humble, to say 'I'm not sure I know how to get there'? Which leader is more successful?" The answer is both of them. You need to be arrogant enough to believe that you can do this and humble enough to know that it's going to be really hard. And if you don't have the arrogance, great. Be humble enough to know that it's going to be really hard and just keep taking that next step.

Mauro Porcini on Humility

One of the characteristics that you need to have is humility. It's very easy, the more successful you are, to fall into the trap of arrogance. The more successful you are, the more you think that you have all the answers. It's so easy to stop listening, to stop questioning yourself, to stop learning. This is the worst thing that can happen to you for one reason: You will stop growing. You will stop planting the seeds that will generate new life and new ideas.

Humility is exactly that. It's keeping yourself in check and understanding for real if you are getting traction or not, if your idea is the right one or not. I want to be challenged. I cannot stand people who keep trying to please me.

Keep practicing humility and questioning yourself. But if you do too much of that, it becomes another risk to find yourself entering situations where you lack confidence. You don't attack. You become afraid. You question yourself too much. This is one of the big problems we see in corporations—lack of confidence, inability to take risks, and the inability to make courageous decisions. The balance between maintaining humility and confidence is key.

SAY YES TO YOURSELF

Failure is a part of creativity. If you allow the fear of failure to stop you, you won't do anything interesting or creative. The only way to avoid it is to not stray from what you know and never push the boundaries. That's the opposite of creativity. Nobody likes to fail. It doesn't feel good. The anxiety can be crippling. Face what frightens you. Making mistakes in the pursuit of your joy and passion fosters creativity. The irony is you can't avoid failure by playing it safe. That could lead to the biggest failure of all, an unfulfilling life.

Amber Rae, author of *Choose Wonder over Worry*, speaks poignantly about not wanting the fear of failure to prevent her from doing what she had always felt driven to do, which was write:

> I didn't want to die with my gift still inside. Yet when it came to my own creativity, I noticed that I was getting in my own way. I had this voice inside my head telling me, "Who are you to do that? Are you good enough? What if they judge you? What if you fail? What will they think of you?" And I really bought into and believed that voice for a period of time, and that was having me play small in my life. I've been writing since I was a kid; it was the biggest dream of all the dreams for me. The things that mean the most to us are also the things that come along with the most worry, anxiety, and fear.

If you want to start a business, the first person you have to convince of its value is yourself. Why are you doing it? If it's just for money, there is a very high likelihood you will fail. It's too hard. It will require too much of you to sustain the effort. If it connects to your passion, you might not make a fortune, but you will feel fulfilled. However, there is another crucial step, as Daymond John told me:

> The proof of concept: Is this just in your head? Does anybody else believe this? That's where you get that confidence when you sell to people. You get feedback, and you say, "They want more." You have to be realistic. If you have goals set, you love what you're doing, and you have a path set that you want to accomplish, you'll get the door slammed in your face many times, but you will also know that's one less road to go down, and sooner or later you'll figure this thing out.

"The door slammed in your face" is a common phrase. It signifies a rejection of whatever it is you are selling. When I was a teenager, I literally did door-to-door sales. If the door was closed before the sale was made, you go to the next door. While I was learning it, it wasn't fun, but looking back, it was an incredibly valuable lesson to learn: There are other doors. What can I do to get through the next one?

It demands that you trust yourself and learn to tune out the negative noise of outside opinions. Fashion designer Brandon Maxwell shared that once he became successful, everyone around him, from investors to publicists, was telling him what to say, what not to say, who to say it to, and how to run his business. With all the noise around him, it became hard to hear his own voice. He learned the survival skills to shelter his creativity from this onslaught by paying attention to one of his best friends, Lady Gaga. It's about the work. It's not about the money or the fame. That kind of focus and purpose is an important skill at any level of creative pursuit—and life. Stay focused on what you are doing. Be who you are. Trust yourself.

However, the only way you can keep going is to believe in what you are doing. I'm going through this as I'm writing this book. I have written a play about Rock and Roll Hall of Fame legend Lloyd Price. It takes a lot of time to research and write it, even more time to get financed, which means selling people on the idea that this play is worth investing in. People ask me if this is a passion project or a commercial. It's both. If I wasn't passionate and didn't believe in the idea, I could never put up with the "doors being slammed in my face." I am passionate. I do believe in it. I know there are other doors. I'm not stopping.

You have to believe you have something of value to communicate. When the response is, "It's not for me" or "I don't think it works," that can be very frustrating. When someone says, "I love this story, and it's important to tell," and they write a check, that energizes me for the next round of knocking on doors.

"It's only disappointing if you don't have self-belief," said photographer Max Vadukul.

When Max was starting out, he met with the legendary *Vogue* fashion editor Grace Coddington to show her his portfolio. She told him his work was "too aggressive" for *Vogue*. When the most powerful creative director in fashion tells you that you don't have a chance there, what do you do? "You could take this philosophy, which I still believe in today," said Max. "Never work where you're not loved. Always go where they love you."

Everyone is going to deal with rejection. I had a meeting with JP Morgan Chase. The first meeting, I thought they loved me. The next meeting, one of the people said, "People think because we're a bank we have a lot of money." I responded, "You are a bank, and you do have a lot of money." The point is that they were looking for reasons to say no.

There are a million ways to say no. There's one way to say yes. They write a check. That's really it. You've got to be aware that this is not about your ego. This is about selling an idea. The only way you can sell something is if somebody pays you for it. It's important because you can lose a tremendous amount of time and momentum by fooling yourself into thinking you were better liked or your idea was better accepted than it was.

It's inevitable. People will say no to you. That's life. But never say no to yourself. When you learn to overcome fear and doubt to explore what you're most curious and passionate about, you never know what's going to hit and maybe even change your life.

What keeps you in the game, and why are you in it in the first place? It's important to believe you have something of value to offer. What is that something? What value does it bring? Rejection and failure will constantly be in your face. It's important to remember you need that one break to keep you moving forward. What's the next idea if the one you just presented doesn't work? If you decide to pick a creative career, you are responsible for its success or failure. A significant part of success is being persistent and not giving up.

Roy Wood Jr. explains:

> There was a guy that was a gatekeeper, and if you got in with him, you got in with six different clubs in the Midwest. He called me and said, "I think you're funny enough. Come on up to Omaha for an audition. I'll give you six minutes." I was thrilled.

Roy drove fourteen hours to do a comedy gig for no money and was excited to do it. These little victories can keep you alive and motivated. He drove fourteen hours, thinking about his jokes the whole way and how it was going to be great. It was. That opened the door. Everything you do leads to the next thing.

IMPOSTOR SYNDROME

Impostor syndrome is a psychological state in which an individual doubts their accomplishments and has a constant fear of being exposed as a fraud. People with impostor syndrome are convinced that they don't deserve the success they have achieved. Thinking that someone's going to find out and take away the things that you've worked so hard for is typical of high achievers. Initially, the syndrome was first studied in high-achieving women. However, according to more recent research by the British Psychological Society, it affects men who are under pressure even more.

For some people, fear is a motivator. Monica Mitro talks about dealing with impostor syndrome. Even at her level as an executive vice president she is afraid that someone will discover that she doesn't know anything. Instead of being paralyzed by those fears, she harnesses the power of those feelings of insecurity and uses them to drive her performance:

I'm always afraid that someone is going to discover that I actually don't know anything about PR and marketing. Fear drives me. Jony Ive [formerly the chief design officer for Apple, who designed such groundbreaking products as the iMac, iPod, iPhone, and iPad] is a close personal friend. He talks about what drives him: "That feeling that someone's coming up behind me, is going to create the next big thing, and that they're going to find out that I'm a phony and I don't know what I'm doing." Even though you do amazing things, you are always thinking that there's someone right behind you who is going to discover something about you; that is what drives me. That feeling of insecurity is actually good. Once you start feeling like "I'm at the top of my game; nobody's as good as me"—that's when somebody just cuts in front of you.

Everybody has doubts. Questioning yourself is good—to a point. If you question yourself too much, you have to ask yourself if you truly have confidence in your own idea. That does not inspire confidence in others about your idea either. This is one of the big problems in corporations: the inability to make a decision and take risks. Ideas need to be challenged. However, it's important to achieve a balance between listening, absorbing other information, questioning yourself, and realizing it's time to commit. Make a decision and move forward.

Paralysis sets in when your inner critic keeps saying, "I'm not good enough. Why should I be doing this?" Where does this inner voice come from? It could be from family, from a teacher you had when you were young, someone who stood between you and the approval you were seeking. It's important to realize that that voice is not you. It's something you got from somewhere else. The question is how you deal with it so it doesn't torture you every time you have to make an important decision.

The first day of class I write the word *wonder* on the blackboard. I change the *o* to an *a*. The word becomes *wander*. When you wonder, it allows your mind to wander. Some people consider that to be a waste of time. I don't. It took me a while to realize how I best work. I wonder about a project. How can I approach it in a unique manner? Why is it interesting to me? What engages me? I allow my mind to wander so I can approach things with a sense of wonder.

Amber Rae began to wonder about the voice in her head that was constantly shouting negative things at her. She went to a gallery and was inspired to start making art, and the voice in her head said, "Art? Who the hell are you to make art?" Amber wondered who the voice was. It was worry. She heard another voice that encouraged her to approach the gallery owner and ask him if they did any art workshops. That voice was wonder.

> I know this might sound crazy. My friend calls my relationship with my inner voices not multiple personality disorder, but multiple personality order because I'm creating order in the chaos of the mind. Many of us share the inner characters: worry, the voice of our inner critic that's constantly saying, "Are you good enough? What if you fail?" Wonder is the curious inner guide, the part that questions worry and says that failure will be a great learning experience.
>
> As long as I'm choosing 51 percent more wonder than worry, so long as I'm still afraid but I'm choosing wonder of what's possible, life takes you on an incredibly wild ride.

NAME IT TO TAME IT

Revealing oneself takes courage. It's a risk, and you assess that risk. Are people going to like me? Not like me? Not care? Robin Williams's mania is what was on display when you saw him in performance. The problems that he manifested and what he revealed made him an amazing comedian. I think it's true in all great art—the artist is revealing something. And that something is also important in terms of creativity because that something becomes your distinctive difference. When you play it safe, you're not presenting any difference. There's nothing terribly interesting about what you're doing. And if you don't take risk, personal risk, you're never going to do anything creative or exciting. But it's very scary to do that.

Amber Rae on
Choosing to Be Safe or True

I had this crystallizing moment while I was writing the book and realized I can write either the safe book or the true book. I had to make a choice because the safe book would have mildly interesting stories, where I'm not really revealing too much, but it might support you in choosing to wonder over worry, or the true book, where I was going to be really fucking raw and go there. And I realized I really had to go all in on one thing. I could feel it when I was writing. That's where I wanted to go. And then the perfectionist inside my head, said, "People might judge you. You can't say that."

I had to do the true book. Whenever I would question myself, I'd say, "Well, is this true? Is this going to reveal in vivid detail an aspect of my soul, and am I turning myself inside out for the benefit of the reader? Yes. Okay, keep going." So long as I knew that was the compass, I could continue to move beyond the voice that would pop up.

One of my strategies is called Name It to Tame It. There's this doubting voice inside my head saying that everyone might judge me and who am I to do this? In my body, that's causing tension in my shoulders and keeping me from moving forward. Neuroscience shows that we can reduce our anxiety by about 50 percent simply by naming how we're feeling. What I like to do is actually name these characters. This actually comes from psychotherapy; it's called parts work.

> *What I've found is that we can negotiate with our doubts; we can negotiate with our fears. So I have anxious Annie and Grace, the perfectionist, and I have all these different inner characters that I've built archetypes around so that when I'm afraid, I can know, "This is fear of judgment" or "This is my fear of not being lovable" and be able to name it, tame it, and continue to move forward. It's not going to go away, but we can shift our relationship with it and not make the fear wrong, but rather just understand it is trying to protect us.*

One of the things that often accompanies doubt is procrastination. I even put off procrastinating. It can be a by-product of fear. It means you don't have to confront these things because you put procrastination up as the firewall between you and what you need to do. "I'm not sure" and "I'm torn" are forms of doubt, which also turn into procrastination. Another form of procrastination is perfectionism. It holds us back from putting ideas out there. Perfectionism is often coupled with a fear of letting go, being vulnerable to criticism or failure. French poet Paul Valéry said, "An artist never really finishes his work, he merely abandons it." We've all heard the phrase "Practice makes perfect." We've also heard "Nobody is perfect." If nobody is perfect, why practice? Since perfection will never be achieved, it is important to learn when to let go and move on. Especially if you are working on a deadline.

There are deadlines that are necessary to meet and deadlines that are self-imposed. Some self-imposed deadlines are motivating, while others become obstacles. Everyone has a sense of where they'd like to be at a certain point in their career, but it's important to be realistic and not punish yourself when things take longer than you'd hoped. Leomie Anderson is a model whose career has gone very well, but not as well as she hoped. I asked Leomie about the obstacles she created for herself:

One of the biggest obstacles I had to overcome in my career is putting a time spot on things. I used to say to myself, "Next season you're going to walk this many shows, and then three months after you should shoot a *Vogue* editorial" or this or that. I'd say to myself, "If within a year I haven't achieved these things, then I'm behind." I put myself in a box and put so much pressure on myself to be able to achieve all these things by this imaginary timeline. One day I just stopped. "I am going to get this thing done, but I'm going to do it in my own time."

I don't know what opportunity is going to present itself that might take me on a different path, but I knew that putting these time restraints on myself was the biggest obstacle, because you're just blocking yourself and you're just making yourself feel bad for nothing. All the things that I wanted do, I've done, but maybe it took three years instead of six months.

A friend of mine, Dianne Benson, brought the avant-garde fashion line Comme des Garçons to the United States and opened their first store. It was designed by Rei Kawakubo, the founder. When the store was opened, there was a write-up by the architectural critic for the *New York Times*. The writer noted a jagged diagonal crack that went across the entire floor. Everything in the store was perfect, but there was this jagged crack. He wrote that only Rei Kawakubo, the designer for Comme des Garçons, could do something like that and disturb perfection so brilliantly, which is how she designs her clothes. Perfection with a flaw. After I read the article, I called Dianne. I had shot Comme des Garçons's American launch. I knew Rei was a perfectionist. Despite the article, I couldn't believe the crack was intentional.

Dianne laughed and said, "No. The temperature dropped to the teens after the concrete had almost dried. It cracked. Rei freaked out, wanted us to redo the floor. We didn't have the money or the time. I will tell everyone it was intentional." Everybody thought it was part of the design. Everybody thought Rei was brilliant, which she is. The crack was a mistake she didn't want. She is a perfectionist, but she could also recognize a perfect story. She just let the story flow. Budget and deadline created a new definition of perfection. A flaw. Flawed perfection. That's what we all are.

Workbook Questions

- How do you feel about speaking in front of groups?

- When have you said no to yourself because of your fear?

- What messages is your fear telling you?

- What practical steps will you take if your worst fears come true?

- When do you find yourself doubting what you are doing or want to do?

- Do you consider yourself a perfectionist? How does that work for you?

- Do you procrastinate? If so, in what kind of situations?

- What can you learn from that?

PART THREE

THE MYTH OF
THE LONE GENIUS

7

Invest in Relationships

I HAD LUNCH WITH NOBEL Prize winners in physics John C. Mather and David Wineland. Mather studied cosmic microwave background radiation, which helped cement the "big bang theory" of the universe. Wineland's work was for "groundbreaking experimental methods that enable measuring and manipulation of individual quantum systems." It was fascinating talking to them. Equally fascinating was their answer when I asked them how it felt to receive the Nobel Prize. They both said it was a great honor, but they both felt strange accepting it. I asked them why. They said that they work with large teams of scientists to accomplish what they do. Everybody's work contributes. It's a bit ridiculous for one person to receive an award when a few hundred should be given out.

From the time we are young, we are told stories about great people who create their works of genius in isolation. I call this the Myth of the Lone Genius. Thomas Edison, the paradigm example of the Lone Genius entrepreneur, had hundreds of people working on his ideas. So did Steve Jobs. The Lone Genius is great for public relations, marketing, and advertising, but recognize it for what it is: a myth. Big ideas can't be accomplished alone. As creatives, we need to surround ourselves with like-minded people who help us broaden our horizons but also function as a system. Having a good team around you is always going to lift you up and motivate you to be better.

SURROUND YOURSELF
WITH THE RIGHT PEOPLE

Relationships are the true currency in life. Who do you want to spend time with? Who will tell you the truth—even if it's not what you want to hear? Who supports you? Who do you want to do business with? Who has capabilities and talents that complement yours?

One of my closest friends is someone I've known since third grade. I said to him, "If I knew the divergent path our lives would travel, I would've never invested sixty years in our friendship. You are of no practical use to me." He laughed. I have close friendships that go back further than that, people whom I'm still in touch with from kindergarten and even before. I have aged, but not matured. We are still friends because we play well together. We can talk candidly. A subset of these friends are those I can call or they can call me anytime when something serious is going down and I or they need support. I call them my 3:00 a.m. friends. These are all true friendships that I value deeply.

In business, on the surface it may look the same, but it's different. There is a transactional basis to the relationship. That's business. Transactions. That doesn't mean you don't enjoy each other, but what brought you together is a transaction. You are useful to each other. There is a distinction between being useful and a friend. There is great value in both kinds of relationships, but business ones usually don't continue if you are no longer transacting. I've had a relationship with Ralph Lauren since 1982. I value it. We have fun together. We do business together. It's a transactional relationship.

A few years ago, I was invited to the Influencers Dinner. At first, I questioned whether I would go. Was it going to be a bunch of people selling themselves and passing out business cards? I figured the worst thing that would happen was I'd spend a few hours, and if nothing else, I'd have a new story to tell—so I went, having no idea what to expect.

I was greeted by Adam Grant, author of the best-selling book *Give and Take*. Adam and I had met the week before at an event. It was a great beginning to what turned out to be a fantastic evening. I met a number of wonderful people: Pulitzer Prize winners, Olympic athletes, artists, writers, and comedians. A number of them have been guests in my class. Since then I've had the good fortune to be invited a number of times. I go every time. The whole idea is getting people together for a robust exchange of ideas.

The Influencers was started by Jon Levy when he was twenty-eight. He is a human behavioral scientist and the author of *The 2AM Principle: Discover the Science of Adventure*. He started the Influencers by inviting twelve people at a time and telling them that they're not allowed to talk about work or give their last name. They cook dinner together, and then when they sit down to eat everybody guesses what everybody else does. You might find out you are dining with one of the actors from *Game of Thrones*, the president of MTV, the editor of *Elle*, a two-time Olympic gold medalist, or a best-selling author. I asked Jon what compelled him to start the dinners.

> I was sitting in a seminar, and the leader said, "The fundamental element that defines the quality of our lives is the people that we surround ourselves with and the conversations that we have with them." If that's actually true, I need to know for certain.

Jon cites a study by Nicholas Christakis and James Fowler where they asked about the obesity epidemic: "Is it the type of epidemic that spreads from person to person?" We've all heard of cold or flu epidemics, but you don't get Alzheimer's because you shook hands with somebody who has Alzheimer's.

A person's chances of becoming obese increases by 57 percent if he or she has a friend who has become obese. Among pairs of adult siblings, if one sibling became obese, the chance that the other will become obese increases by 40 percent. If one spouse becomes obese, the likelihood the other spouse will increases by 37 percent. The prevalence of obesity has increased from 23 percent to 31 percent over the recent past in the United States. Sixty-six percent of adults are now overweight. The increase in obesity is not explained by genetics, and it has occurred among all socioeconomic groups. The scientific evidence supports the notion that phenomena can spread within social networks.

> Obesity spreads from person to person, the way that a cold does. This is also true for happiness, marriage and divorce rates, smoking habits. Anything you could imagine passes through the superhuman organism we call a community or network.
>
> If you want to drastically impact the quality of your life, one of the most critical things that you can do is curate well those around you.
>
> What makes it significantly easier if you want to have a healthier lifestyle? Just surround yourself with athletes. If you want to be more studious, hang out with the kids who are at the library, day in and day out. And their behaviors will inevitably permeate to you.
>
> I decided that if that's the case, I need to figure out how to bring together the most influential people in our culture. How do I get the positive impact that knowing all these people can have? It's the people you curate around you.
>
> I've set out to figure out what engages the most influential people in our culture so they'll actually want to talk to me.

I asked Jon how he got guests and began to establish such a meaningful network.

Everything that I do is underpinned by a basic premise. Anything you want from life is the by-product of two basic factors. Everybody tells you that it's a lot more complex; it's really this simple. It's a by-product of one: Who you're connected to, who knows you exist, and who can you access? And two, how much do they trust you, in that capacity? Meaning, you probably trust me to tell you about a behavioral study. You probably don't trust me to perform neurosurgery on you.

Trust is what's critical. Which means that if we can become expert at connecting with people and building trust with them, there is virtually nothing you can't accomplish.

The fact is that anybody can have connections and anybody can build trust. Which means that if you give yourself a few years, you can build a network, or community of connections, that will allow you to accomplish what you care about.

There is science to back up the way powerful networks can be built. The phrase "six degrees of separation" came from a study called the Small-World Experiment, conducted by social psychologist Stanley Milgram. The goal was to discover the average path length of social networks. The study would test the hypothesis that everyone on the planet is connected by just a few intermediaries, and hence it was called the Small-World Experiment. The test involved a few hundred people from Boston and Omaha. Their mission was to get a letter to a target— a complete stranger in Boston. The caveat was that they could only send the letter to a friend of theirs they thought was closer to the target than they were. When Milgram looked at the letters that successfully reached the person, he found that they had changed hands about six times. The idea that everyone is separated by only six people gave birth to the phrase "six degrees of separation," a phrase Milgram himself never used. New research conducted by Facebook put the number closer to three and a half.

So you are three connections away from a person living in the valleys of Rio, the president, and maybe even Natalie Portman—who knows? But the point is that means that you're not that far from that key person who can impact the quality of your life, or help you accomplish your nonprofit efforts, or meet the person of your dreams. Everybody is that much closer to each other.

How do you start on day one? I took the most influential people that I could, and after each time I'd do a dinner, I'd ask for recommendations.

That is how you build an amazing network like Jon has. It's not out of your reach. There are other ways that are simple and direct and that you can start doing now. When I go to events, I always have my business cards, a pocket-size tablet and a pen because I like to write, and my phone. Jon continues:

Most of the time when you imagine networking, it is one person who knows a lot of people. The strength of this network is really weak because you could lose one person, and then all the connections disappear. But if these people connect, then all of a sudden, the network becomes stronger. In what's called graph theory, which studies the way that networks exist.

A network is strongest when there's a lot of connections, between the points. But here's the added benefit. If this person is really a great person, then there's positive impact on them, and the more people they know, then the positive impact extends. And then you get the secondary effect: if this person's super healthy and happy, this person becomes happier, and then I'm getting this happy person and this happy person is affecting me.

So my objectives shouldn't just be to know a lot of people. It's to bring them together, to form really tight bonds, between them. The reason is twofold. One is that you'll end up in a situation where people ascribe that meeting to you. When things go well, you get the benefit of being remembered, and there's a tight-knit community.

Some people will text you their info immediately as you are talking. Some might not have their phone but have a business card. Others have neither. That's when I take out my pen and write their info in my tablet. There is interesting science backing up the act of actually writing by hand: you remember it better. The goal is to get their information. How you get it is not important. The most important part is what comes next: following up. Don't wait. Be proactive. Some people are great at getting back to you, and some you have to pursue. The main thing to remember is that in most cases, people are busy and you are not at the top of their list, so you may have to remind them—many times. There are different schools of thought on that, but do not take a lack of response personally.

RELATIONSHIPS ARE CURRENCY

Relationships are the true currency in life. I have made money by developing relationships, whether it is clients for my production work or investors in my play. A relationship is the starting point.

One of the people I've worked with a number of times is the stylist Freddie Leiba. Freddie has the interesting distinction of literally creating that career. Before him, that position did not exist. Freddie trafficked in stars. He has worked with many of the iconic designers, magazines, models, and movie stars: Madonna, Beyoncé, Julianne Moore, Charlize Theron, Johnny Depp, *Vanity Fair*, *Elle*, *Harper's Bazaar*, and many more.

I'm dropping names for Freddie because he never would. I first met Freddie on a job for Victoria's Secret. People were telling me who he is and who he knows. There's often a misconception about one's relationship with the talent and celebrities. What is the nature of that relationship? I asked Freddie Leiba if he is friends with them:

No. If they choose to be my friend, that's a different story, but I don't go after them. I'm a client. I don't go there to make friends. I go there to do a job. That's what I'm hired for. I mean, you work with someone and they keep calling you, of course the relationship changes. But I never go with the attitude of becoming anyone's friend. If they come back to me, it's because I did my job. If I didn't do that job, they would go on to the next person. It's as simple as that.

Everyone wants to get famous, not be educated—be famous. I never thought about fame. You have to earn whatever recognition you get. *Fame* is not in the vocabulary at all. It is about your work. I can do a job tomorrow. If I don't show up with the right goods, I'm fired like anyone else.

My career happened because people saw what I did and they appreciated it, so I became that. To be quite honest, just do the work and do it well. Be excellent at what you do. Then it pays off and you stay true to yourself.

You never know who, how, or when you are going to meet someone and a relationship blossoms. Meghan Markle had just landed a part in the series *Suits*. She was going to be doing press for the show and needed a publicist and a makeup artist. The budget was small. Meghan contacted the agency that represented Daniel Martin.

My LA agent reached out to me, and she said there's this young actress, I think you'd get along with her really well. We totally hit it off. When she started [her blog] *The Tig*, that was when we got closer because here's this person who wanted to do something besides just act. That's how our friendship started.

I was just starting my LA residency, being out there for the Globes and the Oscars. It was at this moment where we were both taking that next step in our careers. It was a journey that we shared together. When I found out that she was dating

Prince Harry, I'm like, okay, cool. Going to London and just having your friend's face be on a mask or coffee mug and being on a flag and the whole city was just insane, you're like, fucking holy shit, like this is real.

Daniel forged a great relationship with Meghan before anyone knew who she was. Same with Jessica Alba. I asked him what the key to forming those relationships is. He told me it is listening and understanding the person.

I have to always remember that first and foremost, I am providing a service to these people. If we become friends, amazing. If we don't, we don't. I'm there to take care of the star. I'm not the star. I go into every job like that. I want to make them feel as beautiful as they can be. I have to ask questions. I have to understand, if I'm working with someone new, I go back and look at images of them, what I didn't think looked good on them, and then figure out what makes them most comfortable.

When you're dealing with high-profile celebrities, and I've been in that situation many times, you're forewarned about how to interact. You get prepped by their publicist or PR person, which can set up barriers between you and the person you're trying to establish a relationship with. I asked Daniel what he does to bridge that gap so he can establish a rapport with the talent.

I would say 80 percent personality, 20 percent talent, because at the end of the day, you're trying to make them feel as good as they can. Once you win them over and gain their trust, you can do whatever you want with them in terms of being creative with their makeup. You have to respect their players and just know what you're in for rather than be defensive walking into a job. Just be confident in what you can do, but also be respectful of the environment and who their people are. Because at the end of the day, we're all trying to take care of this person and trying to make them feel as good as they can be. They're just people and it's only makeup. It's not brain surgery. It can come off. If you don't like it, well, take it off. You can't get wrapped into it.

Someone asked me what it took to do good work. My answer: "A client who lets you." EVP of public relations at Victoria's Secret Monica Mitro and I have worked together for many years. It becomes a relationship when there is trust. We have a lot of fun, but it's also about business. From my end, it's making myself indispensable, always offering new things to a client. That also keeps my job interesting because I'm not interested in doing the same thing over and over. I'm interested in doing new things all the time. It's also good business on my part to be coming up with things to keep myself relevant and important. Monica told the class:

> I love new ideas and I love trying new people, but the thing that's kept me going back to Jeff over twenty-four years is that he does good work and he comes up with new ideas. He is like a slot machine of ideas. He and his team come to us all the time with new ideas and new techniques. I always know that if Jeff is with us, I'll get from the day what I need to get because he understands our customer; he understands the changing business.
>
> It's great to work with someone whom you can depend on. That's the other thing because working with someone for the first time is quite scary; you never know what you're going to get.
>
> In any business, you hire people that you are comfortable working with. Everybody works really hard, and if you have a twelve-hour shoot day, you don't want to be around someone that makes your skin crawl, but you still get a good job

out of it. When you're on location, you're with somebody for fourteen days straight. You want to be with people that you enjoy, that you respect. You want to surround yourself with positive energy. It's really key to be that positive person. It is very competitive. There are lots of choices out there.

It's important to remember that it is not just your relationship with the person in charge; it's dealing with everybody around them, being engaged and polite, and showing gratitude. The relationships you build and sustain can have a major impact on your career. It's a truth that cuts across all businesses.

THE CARE AND FEEDING OF RELATIONSHIPS

One of the biggest deciding factors in any endeavor is how you build ongoing relationships with clients and colleagues by constantly adding value.

I've been teaching Creative Careers since 2007. I depend on the generosity of my guests in giving their time and sharing their experiences, and I find good people through other good people. Many of my guests are people suggested and introduced to me by past guests. Personal recommendations are the best way to get guests; it's also the best way to get business. That's why testimonials work. The quality of the referral, based on the quality of the relationship, can lead to business. That is true in all businesses.

I never ask anybody if they could introduce me to someone before they've done the class. The next step is really important: follow up quickly. Don't wait a week or two, as they might not even remember who you are. Following up is important, and that becomes an obstacle for many people—for no good reason. Often, they wait, and then they get self-conscious, thinking it's too late, and then don't do it. Just do it. It's not a big deal. I email them right after they've done the class to thank them. My hope is that they've had a good experience and are happy to recommend people. That is how I've gotten many great guests.

It's important to realize that as well as you might get along with someone in business, it is business first. I'm not talking about your close friends and family. I'm talking about people who have a vested or invested interest in you. Building and maintaining those relationships is crucial.

Be the type of person you would want to answer the phone for. I think a lot about who in my life I love spending time with. True friends bring joy. They're fun. Life is very difficult. Not always, but the fact is that being human is constantly overcoming different challenges. I want to spend time with people I play well with.

You can gauge the value of most relationships by how often you laugh with the person. You can usually tell how much fun someone's having in their life based on how frequently they laugh. Most people don't enjoy their relationships; they endure them.

Joe Polish advises:

> Cut off any ties with people that you're enduring or are a pain in the ass. Don't waste time with people who do not fuel you psychologically, emotionally, or spiritually. There are so many amazing people on the planet, those are the ones that you want to build your businesses with and your futures around.

Relationships not only take time; there is also a give-and-take. Karlie Kloss's career launched quickly. She was wise enough to realize the importance of relationships and how to build them:

> As you pursue your career, you have to understand that you really have to take care of and value the relationships you have. You have to really work on building them in the right way. It's a really small world, so you have to feed and water your relationships.

I went to dinners to support them. I went to events, went to their opening flagship store in New York. It's so much more than just being in the runway show. In relationships, you do favors for people. You give and take, but you have to give to be able to receive.

THERE IS ANOTHER perspective regarding business relationships: You may have started off with an agent who groomed you and built your career to a certain point, but that same agent might not be able to take you to the next level. The business decision is whether want to go to that next level and are you prepared, if necessary, to leave the agent who launched your career. That is going to be hard to do. You built a relationship, but if things hadn't worked out, they would have dropped you and put their energy into someone else. It's important to realize it's your career. That kind of conflict happens all the time. You need to build a relationship with a different agent. It happens to actors, artists, athletes, writers—and it happens to models.

Workbook Questions

- How can you build trust?

- What do you value in a relationship?

- What can you offer in a business relationship?

- Do you follow up with people? If so, how?

- Try your own Small-World Experiment: Can you get to someone you'd love to connect with that you don't know?

8

Creative Collaborations
and Differences

COLLABORATION IS ABOUT WORKING TOGETHER to accomplish a task or achieve a goal. We collaborate all the time, every day. "You wash the dishes, and I'll dry them" is a collaboration. The task is washing and drying; the goal is clean dishes. As the task gets more complicated and the goal harder to achieve, the collaboration can be highly gratifying or frustrating, depending on the people involved and how they are aligned. Creative collaborations can get even more difficult because there are those who are passionate about the goal and others who look at it as a job like any other job. Conflicts arise for all kinds of reasons. The question is what the criteria are for a successful collaboration.

WHAT MAKES A STRONG COLLABORATION?

Celebrity Stylist Micaela Erlanger has a great imagination, so I asked her to pretend I'm Meryl Streep. (In case you are wondering, I look nothing like her.) When you first meet the person you're going to be working with, how does that interaction begin and how do you begin to start thinking about what you should do with this person? What is the conversation? How do you communicate your ideas? How does that collaboration start?

Micaela Erlanger
on Knowing Your Client

It always starts with a conversation. There has to be a natural synergy and sync between two people that are going to be working in such an intimate way together. Keep in mind, these people get undressed. We're working on the image that they're portraying to the world. It's very important, sensitive, and intimate in all senses. It starts with a conversation and then so much research. I like to share images. I like to have inspiration. The inspiration and image sharing and Pinterest boards and magazine tears and scouring Vogue runway. I know what every single collection has. I know what the trends are for the season. I know the beauty trends. I know who has worn what, what's not to be repeated, what will suit a body type. There's so much that goes into it, but it always comes back to that initial conversation.

There's a real psychological aspect of what we do. You have to learn to read a person.

You have to know when it's appropriate to push the envelope in maybe an edgy fashion way or when someone is feeling uncomfortable, how to respect that, respond to that, and dress someone appropriately.

When you're trying to get someone to try something new, be it an idea or an outfit, there is often resistance. Micaela deals with it simply. She tells them to "just try it on. If it's awful, we'll take it off." She knows that some things don't look good on a hanger but are transformed when they go on the body. I asked her about dressing an actress for the Academy Awards or a press tour. Does she have to take the part that the actress played into consideration when outfitting her?

With someone like Lupita [Nyong'o], we love to play into who her character is, and there's a nod to the role in some aspect. When doing Black Panther, *it's a bit more warrior inspired, or for* Star

Wars, *it was a bit more galaxy inspired, or for* Queen of Katwe, *we gave a nod to her African heritage. If the character has a very powerful role and it's a more serious subject matter, I'm not going to put them in something flashy and sparkly because it wouldn't be appropriate for the message of the film that they're promoting.*

Micaela does a tremendous amount of research, and it's not just fashion related. She is constantly watching movies and reading articles about film and the directors. It's all visual. It's all image. There is a lot more to it than putting something cool on a client. In a way, her work is meta; she is dressing an actress for a different part, which may be the Golden Globes or a press junket. The clothing has to make sense in the real-life context in which she's wearing it. She puts together mood boards, which are a great tool for communicating concepts and fostering collaboration. Mood boards can be pictures from magazines or found online, sketches, words, any kind of visual reference put together like a collage to represent the world of the idea you are trying to communicate.

Every client is a little different. Some clients are more fashion obsessed than others. Some need a little bit more help than others, but oftentimes, there's a mood board that's created. Mood boards for my clients are kept private. I know my clients, like Meryl or Lupita, like the back of my hand. I just know what's going to work at this point. I'm thinking for them. It takes the guesswork out of it. It makes it easy, but that doesn't happen overnight and takes time and can't be rushed. It comes with trial and error, seeing how clothes fit on the body, understanding what works, what doesn't, how to turn something that isn't working into something that is, what your client is comfortable with, and so forth.

Then there's also the element of custom design, which I do very often, mainly for big premieres and award shows. I propose sketches probably from two or three different brands, and then the client will choose who they want to proceed with. There's revision of sketches, fabric swatches, a hundred conversations, generally about three or four fittings. You're working with the designer, and they're also providing their ideas; it's very collaborative.

Micaela builds relationships with her clients. Working with people who have a natural chemistry with one another is essential for building a long-lasting relationship. Of course, there are times that doesn't happen. The "initial conversation" is the basis of all collaborations. From the beginning, it's about communication. Good communication is how collaborative relationships are built. Bad communication is how they are destroyed.

Necessity is the mother of invention. Leandra Medine, founder of Man Repeller, combined her creative edit team with her branded content because she didn't have the resources for two different departments. The result of rethinking the creative approach, a synergy was created that not only was great for Man Repeller but also benefited the client. Mutual trust, mutual benefit, is what can build lasting relationships.

Debbie Millman's advice is to always fight for the relationship, not the work. If you put the relationship first, you can have a client for life, while if you put the work first, you'll have one project with that client. She shared a story about designing the merchandising for *Star Wars Episode 2*. When her team first presented their ideas to the client, they hated it. Instead of pushing on stubbornly, she stopped the meeting and said, "Give us another chance to present something you'll like." When they presented for the second time, they liked it much better. But the funny thing was that the final product wasn't significantly different from the first round. By listening and showing she was willing to make changes, she gained her client's trust.

Photographer Terry Tsiolis says that it is important to have the same taste and that you have to respect each other. He is always working with hair and makeup artists. Collaboration is key for a successful photo shoot. "It's like a secret dialogue you have with people," said Terry. "They know exactly what I'm saying. I don't have to explain, 'Make her hair bigger or put more makeup on.' The initial reaction to me with hair and makeup people is just a connection and ease. Obviously, I respect their work, and they respect my work and they know what I want. But then you build together, and it becomes a collaboration."

The more you work with the same people, the more the notion of "a secret dialogue" comes into play. That's why people prefer to work with their own people, because they know the communication is there, even if it's not spoken.

Creative director of *Vogue*, Sally Singer collaborates with photographers, directors, models, and celebrities. The best collaborator is someone who wants to do it, especially someone who is invested in doing something that hasn't been done before. One of her favorites is Serena Williams:

> Serena doesn't just show up because she's Serena Williams, the greatest female athlete. She learns the choreography, she gets her place in that picture, and she does it. You know from the start when you're working with her that you're going to make the thing with her that you've never made before and she's going to be right there for that ride, with a lot of opinions, but it's not like a sheep. The best collaborators are collaborators. Erika Jayne was amazing. We said bring your looks to *Vogue*. Bring your glam squad there. She did it. In terms of photographers and video directors, again, it is people who want to do the thing they haven't done yet, where you go through the work and you say, "I want to go to some place you haven't gone yet."

I was directing a holiday commercial for Victoria's Secret. I came up with the idea of having the models dressed as Santa's helpers, and as they were putting up the holiday decorations they would be singing "Deck the Halls." When I pitched the idea, we agreed that this would be a festive greeting, not meant to sell any particular product. VS agreed.

We submitted the storyboards, our stylist submitted outfit ideas for Santa's helpers, the set designer submitted concepts for the room, the prop stylist submitted the decorations—everything was agreed upon. We sent the models the song. The collaboration was going very well. The communication was clear. The client was happy.

The day of the shoot, the set and lighting looked great. The hair and makeup artists were doing a wonderful job. There were two problems. The models couldn't sing. After all, they are models, not singers. Although some of them grew up with the song, more than half of them didn't. The song wasn't familiar to them. My client was very worried. She took me aside and said, "They can't get through the song; they keep screwing up. This is a disaster. How are we going to get the spot?"

"That is the spot," I told her. The models were always portrayed as flawless beauties. This showed them making mistakes, laughing—like the rest of us humans. I had worked with the models many times before and with VS for years. There was a fundamental trust established that allowed us to go with the humor and have fun with the spot. "Deck the Halls" went on to get tremendous media coverage, which was unheard of for a commercial, and to this day it is the second most viewed video VS has ever done.

HOW YOU COMMUNICATE IS KEY

As a corporate executive for Time, Inc., Fran Hauser places a great deal of importance on nonverbal communication. She believes that 93 percent of having effective communication is about everything other than words. It could be eye contact, posture, smiling when you shouldn't be, the tone of your voice—it all plays a huge part. Fran told me about a board meeting she was in. There was a man who had the floor and kept talking and talking. Nobody else could get a word in.

> I finally just stood up, and just standing makes such a difference because you're taking up more space. It forces everybody to look at you. It gave me the floor, and it was such a simple move.

When you want to show that you're coming from a position of strength, the nonverbal is really important, like the amount of space that you take up. Women tend to take up less space.

It comes down to understanding social cues: tone, body language, facial expressions. That's why you can't just text and email. You need face time with people because you don't know if they're rolling their eyes. You get a text that says, "That was a great meeting and a good idea." If you were talking to them, you might hear a positive tone or possibly sarcasm, irony, humor, or anger. I don't think that we will ever replace that face-to-face because it's so valuable.

In a big company such as PepsiCo, Mauro Porcini has constant meetings, hours of them every day. Often those meetings involve people based in different locations, a design center in Manhattan and multiple offices around the United States and the world. Mauro explained the various strategic ways of communicating within a corporate structure. Because of time and location, the meeting could be a phone call, video conference, or physically in the same room. If he needs to push something, Mauro tries to at least have a video presence, but if the meeting is important, it needs to be face-to-face.

The way I talk, the way I interact with executives, 95 percent of that is the same. But then 5 percent of my tonality and the words that I use changes on the basis of who I have in front of me. This applies no matter if I'm talking at an R&D [research and development] conference, a business conference, or a design conference.

On top of that, my dress code changes. I tell my team that when you are in front of the business organization, they expect you to be creative. They want you to be the cool artist, the one thinking differently. The truth is that if you are just that, they will love you, but they won't see you as one of their peers. You won't be part of the decision-making process.

I have the ability to play with my dress code by managing and balancing the creative cues, so crazy jackets and crazy shoes are some cues that are more familiar to them. I wear a jacket. I wouldn't wear a T-shirt with a Pepsi logo in front of the CEO, for example. They want me to wear a tie. You give them some confidence with cues that communicate business, but then you distract with other cues that communicate diversity of thinking. They want that because they search for diversity, but they also want the comfort and confidence that you understand their world as well. This is also true with your language. The more you are proficient in business, the more you understand strategy, and the more you understand all the so-called boring things of business, the more you can push the envelope with creativity.

The collaborative dynamic at a major corporation or a television comedy show is not far apart. A major difference is that the deadlines are stringent for a daily comedy show. It often takes a long time for a decision to be made on a corporate level. However, in both cases, communication has to be clear and decisions have to be made. In both cases, your idea might get shot down. I asked Roy Wood Jr. to explain the collaborative process at *The Daily Show*. I asked him about his work with other writers, actors, and producers. How does the collaborative process actually work on a day-to-day basis?

Roy Wood Jr.
on Joint Creative Decisions

You have to be open to criticism and critique. Without offense. Because there's just not a lot of room for feelings in the writers' room. Everybody would either criticize it or figure out a way to improve it. It was all on the level. Nobody leaves with their feelings hurt because you brought everything from a place of wanting it to be better. It's no different than a designer bringing something to someone, and they go "Ah, that sucks. I don't like that draft; go back and start again." You just got to go back and start again.

Every day you're going to pitch something. I pitched stuff over email—that's how we pitch at The Daily Show: *we have a morning meeting where all of the writers and executive producers get in a room, and we ping-pong whatever we saw on TV last night, and studio production shows, clips, but then if there's something that you think is funny that should be brought up in the writers' meeting, you can pitch it during the day, and then it gets put on the docket for either the afternoon meeting or the following day. And you'll email something, and sometimes you'll email out an idea on pitch, and it'll be fifteen replies because everybody is adding to it, and it's, you can see your idea blossoming and it's beautiful and it's on TV. And then the next day you can pitch something, and it gets crickets. To the point where I want to reply to my original email and just go, "Really? This isn't funny to you? Y'all suck."*

There are also days when you have to trust your own instincts. A bunch of people might give you some advice—"the joke would be better." We'll go back and forth about a joke for three hours. But at the end of the day, I'm the one that's on TV and has to say it. And if it sucks, I'm the one that's got to go on Reddit and see people saying I suck. So I'm going to do the joke in the way that I best see fit, but you have to be open to that. There are times when I'm dead-ass wrong about what the punch line should be, and I do it at rehearsal and it gets a laugh, and you kind of look up at the writer in the wings and go "Yeah, when we tape later tonight, I'll do the joke the way you wrote it. I'm sorry."

The Daily Show is on four nights a week. They have to make decisions—daily. In a lot of businesses, it seems like it takes forever for creative decisions to get made. Not in this situation. You just have to get it done. It's called "the drop-dead at work." Drop-dead is rehearsal. If it didn't work at rehearsal, it's not going in the show. I asked Roy about the discussion of whether a joke stays in.

We can debate all morning about whether or not to leave this joke in the script, but it goes up at rehearsal. If it doesn't work at rehearsal, that's it. There's nothing else to discuss because you don't have the rest of the day to decide on what is funny. You have three hours between rehearsal to when we tape, from 3:00 to 6:00. You have three hours to figure out what was funny, what is the funniest, so that we can cut the rest of it. If we're talking five-star jokes, you're looking for all the three-star jokes to chop off.

I have been in many meetings with large companies where the executive in charge asks for ideas, then shoots them down, often humiliating the person who brought them up. Of course, the others are quickly discouraged from expressing themselves because they don't want to be in the line of fire. Many top executives confuse fear with agreement. I asked Mauro Porcini how he fosters collaboration and invites people into the discussion rather than intimidating them.

When you work in large organizations, you have a lot of people that push back on innovation for a very simple reason: innovation is by definition risky and inefficient. It's not just about the risk. Any time you do something new, you have tons of inefficiencies in the process and in the cost. If you think about what is required to innovate in a big organization, you start to dilute the impact, the margin, and the profitability of the entire portfolio. By definition, innovation is tough to accept. On top of it, human beings are reluctant to change. It's just not our nature. We preserve inertia. It's the law of the universe. It's how we are. When do we finally change? All these leaders know very well that you need to innovate. You need to change because sooner or later, somebody will arrive and will disrupt your business. Today it's truer than ever because of the world we live in. You need a visionary mind-set. You need a confident mind-set. You need real leaders to drive change.

The design community is, by definition, more collaborative than other communities. I'm not talking about the crazy design "stars"; they make a brand of themselves by not being collaborative, by being insane. Designers are more collaborative for one simple reason: you can have the best idea in the world, but if you don't find somebody to fund it that helps you take it to market, and actually helps you in building a business out of it, you go nowhere. For us as creative people, we always need somebody to help us bring our ideas to reality.

A huge part of any business is leadership and collaboration. What's true at PepsiCo is true in the fashion business. It's true in movies and television. Getting people to align is extremely important in terms of making decisions, getting traction, and moving business forward.

Josh Sapan, the CEO of AMC Networks, is acknowledged as a great leader in the cable and movie industry. He's respected for his ability to involve others and engage others in the decision-making process. (Full disclosure: we've been friends since college.) I've witnessed this during our breakfasts where he'll say to the waitress, "I was thinking of this. What do you think? What do you suggest?" He'll eventually solicit opinions from the surrounding tables before he makes his order for breakfast. He works hard to involve people in the process. I asked Josh how he fosters a fruitful collaborative conversation.

It's a holistic system. I actually do believe in all that stuff. I actually do believe that—what's the Blanche DuBois line? "I've always relied on the kindness of strangers." I actually believe in it. If you ask yourself, "Do you think I'm sort of smart and have some insights?" we'd all probably answer yeah, at least to a degree about ourselves. We're probably either wrong or right because no one's that smart really. Then you say, so if there are another thousand people who are around and they have pretty much as much smarts as we do and you can actually tap them and they're at least as good as you or me, how much better off will you be? A lot better off.

It's not that I'm modest. I just actually observe that people can do things extremely well. We all have strengths and weaknesses, and they're hardly comprehensive. I don't look at it as a nice thing or anything. I just look at it as pure pragmatism, which is if you get people going, you're more likely to succeed because you'll harness their interest and their activity and their contribution. It's very just pragmatic.

PICK YOUR BATTLES

Nothing can become precious to you in terms of your work because you will end up wasting a lot of creative energy defending ideas that are not going to go anyplace. That doesn't mean that you don't stand up and advocate for the ideas you think are really strong, but you also have to realize when you have to let go. How do you determine what creative battles are worth fighting?

Roy Wood Jr. explained:

It comes down to what's at stake. I did this comedy show on BET probably ten, fifteen years ago, and I had a debate with my manager about what my closing joke should have been. We went back and forth, and on the day I decided to make the change to my set and put the joke back in. The joke killed. When I came offstage, he said, "You were right." For me, that was assessing the level of knowledge of the person giving me the advice. I appreciate the advice, but if I'm going to suck, if I'm going to bomb, if I'm going to crash my career into a wall, it's going to be because I chose to do it; it's not going to be off of the decisions of someone else. My instincts are what got me that far, so why wouldn't I listen to my instincts again in this instance? You can go get a second, third opinion, but at the end of the day, for really tough decisions, it's all going to come back to you and what you feel in your gut.

Providing a better solution is key. It's one thing to criticize, but if you criticize and you can't offer anything better, then you're just an obstacle. If you can make a suggestion that might be a better solution, it can possibly move the dialogue forward. These are all critical skills. It's also the art of persuasion. Being creative is realizing there is no one solution. Create a new one. Make the best case you can. Be aware of the reaction you are getting, both verbally and nonverbally, and then leave it to your client to make the final judgment. If you push too hard, they're going to walk away. That's never the goal, unless your ethical principles are being compromised, which is rare in these situations. It's usually about ego.

Michael Arad
on Working with Large Groups

Designing the 9/11 memorial was a huge and historic job. There were many stakeholders—politicians, developers, and other organizations that insisted on weighing in. The selection jury chose architect Michael Arad's design, but the client picked another. It set the stage for a contentious first meeting between the two who were inexorably tied together, the architect and the client.

Nobody wants to be in a confrontational relationship day in and day out. But in some way that energy was helpful because I felt like I got this, and I wanted to give this, and I don't want to let somebody else take over this. Very often that happens: a young designer wins a competition, and then the associate architect will come in and say, "We'll take it from here. You can come to the ribbon cutting."

Michael knew if he wasn't involved, the memorial would become something altogether different by the time it was finished. Another part was the nature of the collaboration. Michael had to transition from working alone to working with a small team to working with so many people. That was a huge adjustment. He also needed the support of his office and partners. It was not just the logistical support; it was also the emotional support. It was an adversarial process with a lot of different people. The issues that came up were significant.

One of the issues we struggled with, late in the game, was that the corners of the pools and the design that we had come to a 90-degree corner. The Mayor's Office for People with Disabilities came to us and said, "Everybody can touch and see the names, but they can't see the void in the middle of each pool if they're seated in a wheelchair. This is two years before this is supposed to open up, and how are you going to modify the design?" A lot of really bad ideas quickly bubbled up to the surface: Why don't you make some panels out of glass? Why don't we put a scissor lift on the Plaza? I couldn't believe somebody actually suggested that a portion of the Plaza go up and down for people in wheelchairs who wanted to see the voided center.

You have to find a way to share your vision with other people, especially people who are in a position to actually make that significant change. You can't just tell people this is important. You have to find a way of showing them why it is important, getting it to be as important for them as it is for you, to have it be their design as much as it is your design.

I asked Michael, on a project so massive, how he determines what creative battles are worth fighting. You can't fight everything. Isn't there a gamesmanship that comes into play?

People will put more inconsequential things in front of you just so that you waste energy on them while they can get something else done. You have to be strategic about what is really important.

When you're in the position of wanting to protect your creativity and your concept, yet you have to deal with a wide range of criticism and opposition, how does he deal with that now that he's been through this process?

I try not to take it personally, which is hard, because we invest our own personhood in our designs. We think, "I designed this." It's like your child and somebody's criticizing your child. I have three kids. They deserve criticism often. Find a way to hear what somebody else is saying. For example, with the names arrangement; I could understand why there was such dissatisfaction with the design I proposed, that sort of the random arrangement, but I also knew that the counterproposal was a terrible idea, too. But the anxiety and the fears that produce that were real. Is there a way to hear what those concerns are and find a different way of responding to it that's meaningful? Don't be inflexible about what you think is important, but also if you're rejecting a proposal, find a way to understand what is at the root of that proposal and find a way, if you can, to address it.

Freddie Leiba meticulously prepares and brings a lot of wardrobe choices to a shoot. He doesn't go to a job to do battle.

We're there to make it work. I have a rack of clothing. If you don't like this dress, that one is fine. Whatever makes you comfortable. As long as you feel good. Madonna wanted Gaultier. I got Gaultier. I go there to solve a problem, not to start one about a dress. I'm not going to fight about a bloody dress. I go there prepared because, of course, it happens. I mean sometimes I put a dress on someone and see it doesn't work. You move on. I always take wildcard options. I bring a room full of clothing when I do something. Completely different things than what they ask for, just in case. You have a conversation. You can meet somewhere in the middle. I listen.

Filmmaker Susan Lacy has a unique method for avoiding creative battles and protecting her creative freedom: a contract. Before she makes any film, she has the subject sign an access agreement. That means they are granting legal permission to make the film so you don't get deep into it and they claim they never said yes to that.

Part of that access agreement is they have no editorial control. They give that away. What I did with Steven [Spielberg] was to say that he could have control over his own interview. I very happily did that because he knew if I put something in the film he wished he hadn't said that he would be able to ask me to remove it. And that way he would be much freer giving the interview and wouldn't be checking himself every second.

He didn't ask me to change a single thing. If you're smart, and they say, "Boy, that person was a real asshole," you don't put that into the movie because you know they don't want the person to know that they thought they were an asshole. It's just good sense. These people are too smart to expect a Valentine, and they know nobody's going to respect the film if it is just a Valentine. It's a portrait. And a portrait involves looking at all aspects of their work. There isn't an artist alive that doesn't have some criticism, and you're not making a balanced film if you're not.

Creative control has to be earned. Susan has twenty-nine Emmy Awards among a slew of other awards. She has proven herself. She is in a position to define the terms of the work she will accept. Most people aren't.

When I met Taryn Brumfitt, she was producing and directing a documentary called *Embrace*. The film explores the serious issue of body loathing, inspiring us to change the way we feel about ourselves and think about our bodies. It was a passionate labor of love, reflecting the struggles Taryn had faced.

Taryn and I collaborated on the shoot. She told me what she hoped to get from the images and the mood she wanted to convey. I asked her what they would be wearing. She wanted to emphasize their bodies and there was no money for wardrobe, so we decided on black leotards against a mottled gold backdrop. She had assembled a diverse group of women: a couple of fashion models and ten others who represented a range of body types, ethnicities, a recently transitioned male to female, and a woman with a physical impairment. Other than the models, no one had been in a photo shoot before.

Their discomfort was palpable. As a director, it is my job to make the talent feel safe. When they feel safe, they will be more expressive and creative. I introduced myself to each one and had a brief conversation. Once they were in wardrobe, I explained what we would be doing. I did the group shot first, so they would have get comfortable in front of the camera, and then shot each one separately. It was a great collaboration with Taryn because after our initial conversation I was free to do what I wanted. All the women were wonderful. Their vulnerability had an impact on me. The shoot was about empathy and humanity. Nothing was being sold. It was a great example of having a well-defined goal, enlisting all the people involved, and executing the concept in a way that everyone was happy. It's great when that happens.

As Freddie Leiba said, "I'm not here to have a battle. I'm here to make it work."

······································

Workbook Questions

- How do you define a collaboration?

- Did you relate to any of the story examples given? If so, which one and why?

- If you offered an idea that was being challenged, how would you defend it?

- In discussions, is your anger triggered when your ideas are not accepted?

- Where do you draw the line in terms of fighting for your idea?

- How do you hope to be treated in a creative discussion?

- How do you treat others?

- Put together a mood board meant to inspire ideas. It could be for a line of clothing, new technology, a movie, or running shoes, whatever you want, but put together images that convey a new concept.

······································

9

Find the Right Collaborators

THERE ARE MANY QUESTIONS TO ask yourself when building a solid team around you when you are starting out in business. Building a team should be very strategic. I've seen companies that staff up quickly and make a lot of mistakes. It's harder to undo problems than it is to avoid them in the first place.

You might not be getting the people that you want today, but you get the best people you can today and upgrade tomorrow. Most companies that scale will tell you that they aren't in the same business they thought they'd be in five years earlier.

This can be a great opportunity for people who don't have a lot of experience but are smart and willing to work their asses off. I'll choose smart, motivated people over those who have a lengthy résumé every time. You can also hire freelancers, until you are sure you have the workload and cash flow to take them on full-time.

One of the big problems for a lot of businesses, especially start-ups, is wanting to attract talent that you can't afford. How do you attract that talent, and how else can you compensate them? Awarding equity at a certain point can be a big incentive for some. According to Dennis Crowley:

> There are the folks that you get very early on that are like, "I make a ton of money at Google, but I'm willing to take

a pay cut because I want an equity ownership stake in your company," which we give and we'll give them a lower salary. We'll give them the benefits the company can afford. It's really hard to compete with Google, Facebook, and Twitter because they're public companies. The stock they can give employees is liquid, meaning they can sell it. They can make money off of it in a way that as a private company we can't do right now. The cash compensation is often a lot larger at these bigger established companies, but you're not a cog in a machine. You are the machine. You're the one guy that's responsible for making this whole thing work. People like that responsibility, and they like stepping into those roles.

There are other challenges. When you are starting out, most often you don't have the cool office or the client roster to attract the kind of people you want. However, if your business grows, you may get the cooler space and higher-caliber clients. That doesn't mean your problems are over—it means they've changed. A constant I've heard and experienced is that it's hard to find smart, hardworking people even if you're paying them a lot. It's important to have perspective, especially if you are a founder. Stephanie Jones agrees:

No one's going to care about your business as much as you, but hopefully you will find people who are close to that. It's hard in the beginning. You really have to work at it. And you have all these jobs, and you work all these crazy hours. You're HR [human resources]. You're CFO [chief financial officer]. You're accounting. You're hiring and firing while dealing with all the clients. It's a lot of emotional work because it's yours, and you have ownership of it. You have moments where you're like, "Oh my God, this is the best thing I've ever done. I'm so happy. This is the best day ever." And then the next day you want to jump out of the window because every client has a crisis or there's drama with two people at work. Shit hits the fan, and then two or three other things happen that same day. There are definitely peaks and valleys.

One of the things that impressed me about Kathy Ireland's company was the longevity of some of her key people. I asked Kathy how to keep good people. She replied:

I think when you consider others as more important than yourself, which is counterintuitive, but when we really think about how we can be of service to the people who are working with us, you build these lasting relationships. There are also partnerships that you can offer. They may not be "legal" partnerships, but they can be emotional and financial ones, or some kind of incentives where in success, they're going to rise along with you. That motivates people to do well.

Randi Zuckerberg told me how hard it is to attract high-level people based on the perception of what someone will cost and how to work around that:

That's why so many start-ups skew young. Unfortunately, there is a bit of ageism in the start-up community because anyone who is established enough in their career is immediately deemed to be too expensive. Experience comes with a lot of dollar signs, and a lot of start-ups get nervous about that. What a lot of start-ups do to combat that is they give equity. A lot of the advisory work that I do for companies is for equity trade. Also, start-ups can take on some of those experienced people as advisers first and then work them into a more permanent role in the company as it ages.

I'm a big fan of giving equity to people, especially in the early stages of a company, or people who can add value. I don't think you should give up so much equity that you lose control of your company. It's your company. In order to retain control and decision making, you need to be the majority shareholder in the company, but the only way you're going to get employees to stay with your company is if they feel like they're invested for the long term. You want experienced, strategic advisers and partners who are going to open their Rolodex for you, who are going to make those great introductions, because it's going to benefit their wallet as well.

The necessary skills for small and large companies are different, yet each one is valuable. Larger companies need to build larger teams. There are more personality factors to consider. In larger companies, things get political. It's important to have the skills to navigate those situations. In smaller companies, it's often necessary to wear many hats because what's required today or even this morning is completely different from what you'll need to do later. I strongly believe you find good people through other good people. As the director, my right-hand people on set are the cinematographer and assistant director. I let them pick their crew from people they've worked with before. The worst thing you can do is force someone to work with people with whom they have no experience. The other key part of them hiring their own crew is that it eliminates any excuses based on crew incompatibility.

As a business grows, there are more challenges that can affect the culture of your company.

Ben Parr, author, journalist, cofounder and CMO of Octane AI, shared his observation:

> You'll find out as the company grows, where initially you know everybody, and you might even refer to each other as family. Now I don't refer to my team as family, not because I don't feel some of that sentiment but because companies are not families. Let's be honest about that. You're going to end up firing people, and you don't want to be telling someone "you are family" and then fire them next month because revenue numbers were missed. It's not family. That sounds cold, but it's also less cold

to be honest about that. It's a company. We do really adore each other, but we have to hit metrics; we have to survive. As a result, it is possible that even if regardless of what your performance was, I may have to reduce team or I may have to fire myself. Don't fall into the trap where your company is everything, especially if you're not the founder. Think about what is best for yourself, and likewise think about how can I help the company, but don't do it at the expense of yourself and your career. Blind loyalty is never a good thing.

TAKING THE LEAD

I got a job in a family shoe store in Summit Mall, the newest shopping mall near Akron, Ohio. The job listing was for someone over twenty-one, married, with at least two years of retail shoe experience. I was single. Never sold a pair of shoes—and I was sixteen. I interviewed with the manager. We hit it off. Everything seemed to be going great. Then he said, "You seem like a great kid, but you don't fulfill any of the qualifications for the job. I like you. I'd love to hire you. I can't. Sorry." I said, "I sold you, didn't I? That's got to be harder than selling a pair of shoes." He laughed but said he couldn't do it. I left his office and was about to exit the store when he called out to me. "You've got the job." He told me, "I am a lot harder to sell than a pair of shoes. You've got the job." We shook hands. "Congratulations," he said.

Bob took a risk and hired me—and I did not want to let him down. I was often the highest-grossing salesperson. Although he mostly played it by the book, the shoe store was part of a chain and had established policies. He also used his gut and did what he thought was right. The way he led had a big impact on me.

At the back of the store was a cage with a spider monkey. The idea was the kids would go watch the monkey while their mom tried on shoes. In theory, it seemed like a good idea to the owners of the chain of stores. They had a monkey in every one. In practice, it was horrible. The kids teased the monkey. The monkey, for good reason, hated the kids. I'm sure these days there are humane-society rules that would prevent having a caged monkey in the back of a store.

At the end of the day, the assistant manager, Jimmy, told me to clean out the monkey cage. I looked at the five other salesmen standing around and asked if everyone else took turns cleaning out the cage. "No. That's your job," he told me. I refused. Bob, the manager who hired me, heard us and asked what was going on. Jimmy told him I was refusing to clean the monkey cage. "I'll take my turn if everybody has to do it, but it's not *my* job. I was hired to sell shoes, not be a zookeeper."

"It's your job if I tell you it is," Jimmy insisted.

Bob handed Jimmy the keys to the cage. "It's your turn. You can show Jeff how to do it. We will all take our turn."

Bob was a good leader because he did so with authority and fairness. He not only led but also followed. He listened to the people who worked for him.

There are bookshelves, and probably dumpsters, filled with tomes about leadership. Some are great. Some aren't. What I found most insightful were the candid conversations I've had with people who are in leadership positions. Simon Sinek thinks a lot about leadership and deals with leaders of all walks of life, from Fortune 500 companies to the military. We spoke about his unique vision of what makes a great leader.

Simon Sinek on Leadership

I am a student of leadership, of being human. Good students study and learn and have teachers and coaches. It's a student mind-set. You show up to learn no matter how senior you are. The best leaders I've met, they're like little kids. They're so curious. They hang on your words. They don't necessarily agree, but they want to know what you think.

Leadership has nothing to do with rank. That is a leadership position that is not a leader. I know many people who sit at the highest levels of organizations who are not leaders. They have authority, which is why we do as they tell us because they have authority over us, but we would never choose to follow them. Yet I know people who have no rank and no authority that have made the choice to look after the person to the left of them and made the choice to look after the person to the right of them, and they are absolutely leaders and we would follow them anywhere. Leadership has the responsibility to see that those around us rise. Leadership has the responsibility to see that those around us are in an environment where their passion glows.

Leadership has a responsibility to create an environment in which we release the passion and other people to see that they work at their natural best to create an environment in which they feel safe being themselves. That's what it means to be a leader. You can be a leader to one person, and they can work next to you, above you, or below you. Do you have to be a leader in the company? One hundred percent, you do. Do you have to be an authority or have a position of rank in a company? Absolutely not. Do you have to even be ambitious to have a leadership position in a company? Absolutely not. But the choice to be a leader is the same choice as being a better version of a human being. If the question is, is it important to be a better version of myself—should I be a better human being? Of course. Then you become a leader.

The qualities of leadership are gender agnostic. My mom and dad were independent business owners. Part of dinnertime was them discussing business decisions. That was a long time ago, when there weren't many female business owners. My dad took a lot of criticism from people who said, "Why do you make your wife work? Don't you make enough money?" My mom would tell them, "I work because I want to work. I enjoy what I do."

Men were respected for being tough, strong leaders. Women who had the same traits were denigrated and considered ball-busters. There was a template set for business leadership that still exists. Steve Jobs, who is reputed to have been incredibly harsh to everyone, was excused for his behavior because he was a brilliant visionary leader. Look at the toxic culture of Uber. The qualities of kindness and strength are difficult to fold into business culture, but they don't have to be.

Fran Hauser, a venture capitalist and the author of *The Myth of the Nice Girl*, told me:

> The most effective leaders lead with both kindness and strength. You know you can be caring but still have high expectations of your team, right? You can get input from people when you're making a decision, right? Be inclusive, but at the end of the day, stand firm in your decision. There's this myth that these things are mutually exclusive, and they're not.

It's only recently that the concept of corporate leadership is beginning to evolve.

THE STUPID QUESTION IS THE ONE NOT ASKED

I've been in so many meetings and heard so many things that made absolutely no sense, but people are reluctant to ask questions. Many other people around that table often have the same question but aren't comfortable speaking up. That is a trait of a bad corporate culture. People are afraid to ask because they might be humiliated or shot down by leadership.

Communications executive Maura McGreevy said she was surprised as she got into more of a leadership role about how people became more afraid to ask questions:

> It's really debilitating for an organization if there's nobody in the room going, "Why are we doing this? Can someone explain to me what the backstory is here? Who are we really trying to reach?"
>
> Ask questions, especially when it's something that's kind of big or overwhelming. Be the person who helps better focus the conversation. Everyone will be better for it. Other people have that same question, and they're just afraid to ask. Be the person who's brave enough to say, "I don't get it."
>
> My boss at Thomson Reuters was so good at that. This powerful, brilliant woman who in the most senior-level meetings would say to the CEO or a board member, "Can someone explain this to me in plain English?" She was a senior executive who could just as easily have pretended to have all the answers. But there she was instead asking questions.
>
> It was shocking to watch how that would change the conversation because half the room didn't know what we were talking about, either. She helped us all better understand. If you're in a communications role, being that kind of truth seeker will only make it easier for everyone to succeed.

Asking questions helps clarify the task at hand, and it helps form a bond among the people in the room because they felt the same way and now the issue is being addressed.

People are afraid to ask questions because they don't want to sound stupid. They want to be liked. The only stupid question is the one you don't ask that screws you up down the line.

Dorie Clark has written about the distinction between competence and likability, which plays into getting a job and then moving up the career ladder and into leadership. I asked her about the research she has found in this area.

> In widely repeated research, it turns out that among both men and women, if you are perceived as being extremely likable, you are typically perceived as being less competent. It's known as the "Likability Conundrum." That's awful because why can't you be likable and competent? We're wired to a certain extent to assume that they are inversely correlated. If somebody is extremely likable, we assume that they may be a little stupid or not able to get the job done. This disproportionately affects women because women are typically socialized to be highly likable.
>
> This prized trait in women generally puts them in a conundrum: if she is seen as highly competent, oftentimes her likability plummets and she gets penalized for it. There's no one in the world who thinks that Hillary Clinton is incompetent. The people who don't like Hillary Clinton think she's mean and conniving. They say Donald Trump thinks she's crooked, but nobody thinks that Hillary Clinton can't get the job done. Everybody knows she's competent. But many people perceive her as not being likable. The trap here is that it is a great thing to be likable.

The question is how you walk that line of being nice but also wanting to be taken seriously.

Fran Hauser told me about a study done in the *Harvard Business Review* where they examined likability and competence.

Fran Hauser on Being Nice

The myth is that if you're too nice at work that you're not going to get ahead, that you're not going to get the corner office, whatever the corner office might mean to you. You can communicate both kindly and directly. You can be both ambitious and likable. There's a myth that you can't do both.

I wanted to make sure to communicate that you don't want to veer into people-pleasing territory because I think that's when you get into being a pushover and being taken advantage of. There are very subtle differences. Like it's great to be helpful, but you don't want to be subservient, because you self-sabotage when you're subservient. Think about being nice, kind, empathetic and compassionate, and also being strong.

What they found was that if people have to choose who they're going to work with, they would rather work with somebody who's likable over somebody who's competent. Ideally, it would be both, right? You would be likable and competent. That's what we should all aspire to be. But if people have to choose, they're going to go with a person who's likable, and it makes sense. The best jobs that I've had, the first thing that I think about is the people that I worked with and how much I loved working with them.

Google looked at their best-performing product teams because they wanted to figure out what was the common thread among those teams. What they found was that the best-performing teams all had one thing in common. The people that were on those teams all had a huge amount of respect for each other. When you respect each other, you create a psychologically safe environment so that people feel comfortable disagreeing; they feel comfortable speaking up and voicing their opinion. It all came down to psychological safety. This is a huge tech company; it wasn't like they found the teams that were the best performing were also the best coders.

When you are kind to people, they trust you, and when they trust you, that allows you to develop a relationship. Being successful in business is all about relationships. That's the power of kindness; it allows you to develop those relationships that can be really helpful to you in your career. There is also so much power in empathy; if you talk to any negotiating expert, they'll tell you that the most important thing when you're negotiating is showing empathy, trying to get into the other person's head and understanding what they value.

The thing that I struggled with the most was that I was told by certain managers or mentors that I needed to develop more of a tough persona, in order to be successful. I kept hearing over and over, "You're too nice. You smile too much. You need to be tougher."

When I was at Coca-Cola I was twenty-six, and my boss promoted me into this really big role over people who were in their forties and had so much more experience than me and had been at Coke for much longer. He said the reason he promoted me was because I was able to influence people. I had built a team that was loyal to me, built really strong relationships, and I had a strong network. He talked a little bit about my technical skills, but he talked more about my relational skills. That was the moment where I was like, okay, this is working for me, and I'm just being myself. It's the reason I got this big promotion. That moment gave me a lot of confidence to continue to be who I am and bring that to work.

In the late 1930s my mom became not only the youngest but also the first woman to become the head of an entire floor at the department store where she worked. She was smart, funny, and well liked. She was well over four feet tall, four foot ten and a half to be exact. She was much taller in stature. Shortly after her promotion by the store owner, one of the male executives told her to fire a couple of the women in her department. "They are good employees. Why should I fire them?" "Because I told you to" was his response. My mother told him, "No. That's not a good reason. I'm responsible for this department. I'll determine who gets hired and fired. You want to fire them, you'll have to fire me first." He backed down. My mom had the highest sales of any employee week after week. She was promoted by the owner. She knew her position. The executive had challenged her in front of the other employees in her department, trying to cement his position of authority. His position was cemented, but not in the way he had hoped. By being a kind and strong leader, my mom earned the loyalty of those who worked for her.

YOUR PERSONAL BOARD OF DIRECTORS

It's important to have people in your life who will give you wise counsel and are concerned about your well-being but aren't necessarily a day-to-day part of your business. Regardless of the size of your business, mentors can enrich your life by helping you make smart decisions, recognize opportunities, and sort through difficult times.

A relationship with a mentor is founded on a mutual sense of trust and responsibility. It's about building a relationship, and relationships that are meaningful require work.

Richelle Parham, managing director of WestRiver Group, advises developing what she calls "a personal board of directors"—a group of people who know her well whom she can go to with a particular challenge, question, or opportunity:

> I put opportunities in front of my personal board of directors, and they give me their opinion of what they believe I should do based on all the things they know about me. That doesn't mean that I'll take any one of those people's advice, but the collective of what I hear helps me make the decision.

Daymond John said that businesses are three to one more likely to succeed due to mentors, especially mentors who have no interest in your business. He sees that all the time in *Shark Tank*.

Whether it is an individual mentor or putting together your own personal board of directors, there is a lot to be gained from seeking outside expertise, and you can approach it in different ways. The majority of people I've interviewed have mentors who have helped them navigate their career.

A mentor can give you advice about how to approach political situations. They can give you advice about whether you should seek outside financing or what you should be charging for what you do. There are connections that can be made that can be tremendously helpful. It's important to realize that it doesn't have to be just one person. Cultivate your own personal board of directors with a range of expertise who can bring value and challenge you. Having people you can seek counsel with in a candid way can not only help you in business, but also help diminish the stressful feeling that you are alone and that nobody understands what you are going through but you.

On Mentors

The way that I define [mentor] is finding somebody that inspires you, that you can relate to, and that is giving you an opportunity to share knowledge with you. My mentor was my boss. She was like a big sister as well. It's based on the foundation of trust, of mutual respect, and that's not something that's inherently given to you. That's something that's earned, takes time, and has to come with making yourself invaluable and really developing a relationship and a rapport with somebody. I worked with her for a year. I proved it. I earned it. In return, she gave me that mentorship. It was extraordinary.

—MICAELA ERLANGER

With mentors, find people who you admire, respect, and want to learn from. If you don't know them, I encourage you to do what you can to try to meet them. Call them, stalk them a little bit. I don't want you to get a restraining order, but if they've written things, read about them, learn from them. Write to them. You can be mentored by somebody you've never met by reading about them. Be curious and ask questions. When you find somebody, just ask them if they'll mentor you. That can mean different things to different people. Some people really like in-person mentorship; for other

> *people, it's a phone call every once in a while, checking in. Find*
> *someone who will keep you accountable. Please don't surround*
> *yourself with "yes" people because you'll never grow with that.*
> *Find people who love you enough to tell you the truth. Even when*
> *it hurts. Hopefully, they'll do it in a kind way, but you need the in-*
> *formation if you're going to grow and get better.*
>
> **—KATHY IRELAND**
>
> *I struggled for a while finding mentorship and a network because*
> *there are just not that many women in tech. I didn't have that many*
> *women to look up to for guidance or that many women around me.*
> *One of the things that I did, I started finding women who were my*
> *peers in other industries that were male-dominated industries. I*
> *connected with women in finance, with women in Hollywood, and*
> *all of a sudden, I had a really strong peer network of women who*
> *weren't sitting right next to me in Silicon Valley but were going*
> *through many of the same things and could offer advice. One of*
> *the things I learned is that we waste a lot of time searching for that*
> *high-level mentor that's going to fix all of our problems when your*
> *best mentors are often sitting right next to you as your peers.*
>
> **—RANDI ZUCKERBERG**

A lot of people struggle with asking people for help. They perceive it as a weakness. They think they should be able to figure it all out on their own. We all have strengths and weaknesses. We all need help. It is not a sign of weakness to ask for help. It's being pragmatic. There is no such thing as the Lone Genius in business. Knowing what you don't know is as important as knowing what you do. Determining that is a necessary skill. Putting together the right team is another. You have to be part psychologist because you need to understand what people want and need. Sometimes they can't articulate it. Putting together a great team, especially when you are trying to do it without much money, is difficult. Approach team building like an opportunity, but first you have to define what that opportunity is and what it means to the person you are trying to attract.

Lead people like you'd want to be led. It's as simple and as complicated as that. We pick up cues on leadership from the time we are kids. We learn from our parents, teachers, coaches, and jobs. Sometimes we have to learn new things to move forward.

Seeking outside help in the form of mentors, creating your own personal board of directors, is a fantastic way to learn and expand your brain trust. However, you can't just take. What can you give back? Asking someone if you can "pick their brain" is not an attractive proposition. I've been asked that many times. The expression creates an image that is not appealing: vultures. I don't want my brain picked. I am happy to help. Gratitude is a form of reciprocity.

Workbook Questions

- What talents do you need around you that are both necessary and complementary to yours?

- What are your weak spots, and how can you find collaborators who are strong in those areas?

- How are you willing to compensate them?

- Who do you know with skills different from yours that can serve as part of your personal board of directors?

- How can you find those people?

- Are there people around you with whom you can build a relationship in order to learn from them?

- What can you give back to them in return?

- If there is no one you have access to now, are there people you admire that you can read about or study?

PART FOUR

THE POWER OF STORY

10

Tell a Story About Your Creation

IN 1991 RALPH LAUREN WON the CFDA Lifetime Achievement Award. It is the most prestigious award a designer can win, considered to be the Oscar of the fashion industry. Consistent with Ralph's love of the movies, the award was going to be presented to him at a gala black-tie event at Lincoln Center by Audrey Hepburn, a true movie legend. Ralph wanted me to do the video. We went through his vast photo archives of beautiful ads. There were pictures of Ralph and his family, all posed beautifully on horseback with mountains in the background. I wanted something more personal to be included. I asked him if he had any personal photos or videos.

He invited me to dinner at his home with his wife, Ricky. He had photo albums that dated back to his early childhood, including a stunningly cute baby picture. I told him I wanted to use those. He said no. I said that I wanted to surprise the audience and show him how they have never seen him. He said no. I told him I wanted to show his humanity, not just the beautiful images from ads, him, as a kid, as a young married man, as a father. I wanted to show his life. No.

"I want to show you something," I said. I remembered I had the video I had just edited for my parents' fiftieth anniversary surprise party in my pack. I put the cassette into the player and watched Ralph and Ricky watch it.

"I'm crying, and I don't even know these people," Ralph said.

I told him, "That's what I want to do for you."

He agreed. I put together the video and presented to him when I was done. He cried. That's Ralph's barometer. If it touches him deeply, it works—like a great story. A movie.

The night of the event, as I sat watching Audrey Hepburn introduce my film, I knew it would either be a big success or crash in the first few seconds. The fashion crowd and movie crowd are a tough audience. The room darkened. The screen fades up to Ralph's unmistakable face, as a baby. There was a gasp from the audience. They were completely surprised and completely engaged. Near the end of the film, as Ralph triumphantly walked the runway, I intercut shots of his past and what led him to where he is now. The audience was on their feet cheering and applauding and continued to do so as Ralph walked out to receive his award. The film worked. The story was told.

Storytelling goes back to our most primitive roots. Somebody had to explain something to somebody. Those who had or at least seemed to have the answers attracted more people to listen to their stories. The size of their audience reflected their position of authority. Shamans were storytellers who created the illusion that they controlled the weather and were somehow connected to a higher power to see into the future. Religious leaders told stories that made sense of the world. Story is the medium through which we communicate. It has the power to bring us together or tear us apart. It also has the power to sell us something.

WHAT STORY DO YOU WANT TO TELL?

In the first half of the twentieth century, Konstantin Stanislavski, the Russian theater actor and director, developed a revolutionary approach for actor training that came to be known as "The Method." Previously, it was thought that vocal and physical training was all an actor needed. Stanislavski went much deeper, involving the motivations of the character and an understanding of the world they were living in, in order to create believable characters. The world and all the existing conditions are what influence behavior and determine who that character is, how she lives, and what she wants forms the "given circumstances."

Although "given circumstances" is a dramatic construct, it is also a great organizing principle for your project and brand. When starting any creative project, it's essential to ask yourself *what* you are trying to communicate and why. What is the goal of the story you are trying to tell, and what are you trying to accomplish? When we go to live theater or see a movie, the actors are the vessel for the story. We have to be convinced to go along with it, but when it's effective, they are "selling" us a reality that keeps us engaged, entertained, and sometimes inspired.

For example, let's look at James Bond. He lives in a world where no one can be trusted. He lives by his wits and physical toughness. He is fearless and relentless in his mission, which is usually to save the world from some catastrophe plotted by a power-mad and wealthy villain. This defines how he behaves in any circumstance. James won't give up information if you torture him and doesn't back down from a fight. But he is not a superhero. James can't fly like Superman or have blades eject from his knuckles like Wolverine. Those actions don't fit within his "given circumstance," that is, the world he lives in. The given circumstances determine how the actor playing James and all the other actors will behave. The given circumstances are created by the writer. They also inform the production design and wardrobe departments; James Bond doesn't wear baggy jeans and a plaid flannel shirt. He doesn't vape. He always looks stylish and cool. He doesn't drive a generic car or wear a generic watch. James Bond not only is a heroic fictional character but has become a brand. His image sells cool cars and expensive watches. Storytelling creates the opportunity to build a brand and sell products.

For example, Apple's brand is a story about hip innovation and cool design. Like James Bond, the given circumstances for Apple products help them determine what products to make and how to promote them. Looking through the lens of storytelling can not only help you organize your thoughts but also create a compass for your business. Apple does not sell their products' features; there is no technical information in their commercials because people don't retain the facts. But they remember the story. Their stuff looks cool, and people use it in a cool way, like walking up the side of a building when you are listening to music you downloaded from iTunes onto your iPhone. You become part of that cool world when you buy it. That's the story, and stories appeal to the emotions of the consumer.

There was no market for filming fashion shows when I started. I couldn't point to other companies who had success doing what I was doing. I had to establish a proof of concept by selling the idea of filming the shows and then getting hired to do it again and by other clients. That's what happened. Halston hired me. Since he was so influential in the fashion world, other designers saw what he was doing, and I got more work. The proof of concept was established; someone bought what I was selling, and bought it again, and others followed suit. You can't just think you have an idea that can make money; you have to prove it. However, I was not soliciting outside investors where proof of concept is essential to attract financing. I had to prove to myself I could make a living doing what I wanted to do.

PROOF OF CONCEPT

What is proof of concept? It is nothing more than coming up with an idea about doing something unproven and showing other people that it is viable. Usually, it is viable because there is an audience for it—meaning people are buying it. Daymond John describes it this way:

Proof of concept is simple: you have an idea, or a product, and you present it to the market, and actually sell it. If the concept works well and it's something that can be repurchased, you sell it again and again. The first initial concept is going to be how many did you sell and in what amount of time? What price was it? Did people reorder this product? Did they come back for it? What was the feedback? Were they absolute strangers? That's what proof of concept is.

Documentary filmmaker Susan Lacy faced a different problem when pitching her idea for a PBS series that would feature biographies of important people in popular culture. "If this was such a good idea, it would have already happened." They said that no one is going to watch documentaries about artists in prime time. They were going to air it at 2:00 a.m.

There was no audience at two o'clock in the morning. So I said, let's create a place for it in the same way that we've created a place for *Great Performances* and a place for science with *Nova*. Let's create a biography place and see how it goes. The show was *American Masters*. By the time I left, I had produced 215 documentaries, created a place for them on television, and won twenty-seven prime-time Emmys. It changed the television landscape.

Whatever product or service you are selling, proof of concept is necessary. If you look at PBS as a major retailer, it's about getting good display space. How do you get prominent positioning so that people will see what you're putting out there and respond to it? If you're all the way in the back of the basement of the store, you're not going to generate consumer traffic. If you get on prime time or if you get on the main floor or you get a window, people come in. I'm pointing this out because it is one of the recurring themes in the book: All businesses are the same. The obstacles you have to overcome are the same. Getting your work financed, getting your work seen, those are the same challenges whether you're making a film, designing clothing, or writing a book. Whatever it is: It's airtime, it's the display space online, it's shelf space. It's all of these things in order to get an audience to see it.

So how do you accomplish that? By learning how to pitch.

POWER OF THE PITCH

My crew was shooting backstage during the Victoria's Secret Fashion Show in 2007. The Spice Girls were performing. I saw the models dancing and singing along with their music. It clicked. I knew there was something there. I had a couple of my cameramen focus on the models singing and enjoying the music. I used bits of it for the promotion of the show, which was going to be on CBS, but I knew there was a bigger idea I could pitch. Each year Victoria's Secret had a major musical guest. I thought it could be great to shoot a music video where the models lip-synch and dance to the song; it would promote the show and the artists' song, so they would be willing to grant the rights. We edited a thirty-second video of the models doing their dance to the Spice Girls' music. I pitched the video and its potential benefits for the brand to Monica Mitro, a co–executive producer of the show and EVP of branded entertainment and events for Victoria's Secret. She loved the idea, saw the value in it, and gave the go-ahead. We did videos with the music of Justin Beiber, Taylor Swift, Katy Perry, and Maroon 5, each one being very popular, trending on YouTube and promoting the show.

Having the idea is only the beginning. Being able to present a video that clearly illustrated what I was pitching, along with presenting the benefits for the brand, made it a hard-to-resist proposition. A key part of the pitch was telling the story of what I saw backstage: the fun the models were having with the music, and how it united fashion, entertainment, and music with the models as the stars—which was consistent with the goal of the show.

A pitch is a form of story. It has a beginning, middle, and end. The audience for the story is someone who can buy the product, service, or invest in the business being pitched. To engage, a pitch needs to be concise, informative, and entertaining.

The pitch as mass entertainment became a phenomenon in 2009 when the Emmy Award–winning series *Shark Tank* premiered on ABC. According to *Shark Tank* shark Daymond John, there are a few key elements to an effective pitch:

1. Can you relay it in a timely manner?
2. Can the person you're pitching to resonate with the need for it?
3. What's in it for the person you're pitching?

Number three is the most important aspect, Daymond stresses, because the person you're pitching may not want to make more money. They may want the social value of what's in it. They may want to work with you because you happen to be a younger or different generation and they can learn from you. They may want it because they want to be cool and they want to be part of this movement. They may want it because they love art and you happen to be very artistic, or they may want it for money. But what's in it for the person you're pitching?

Daymond has seen so many pitches and competed with other smart businesspeople that I asked if there had been any major takeaways from his experiences being pitched and the responses of the other sharks.

"Yes," said Daymond. "Money is not going to cure it all, and people are who we invest in. Those are the major ones because so many deals have been done that have not worked, not because of lack of capital. It was the lack of the person who was running the company." I asked Daymond if, knowing what he knows now, he would have invested in young Daymond John. He paused for a moment, and then said, "Nobody has ever asked me that before," nodding his head, and he said, "Yes, because I saw that kid out there every week selling knit caps out of the back of his car, and he usually sold them out. Proof of concept. Yes. I would invest in him."

You're always pitching every single minute of the day. You're not pitching when you just talk to an investor. The due diligence with an investor doesn't start when you pitch. It starts when you walk in the room, late, early, disheveled, put together. Ready. Confident.

A pitch is a pitch, no matter what you are trying to sell. Sarah Maslin Nir not only had to pitch herself to get a job as a writer but also constantly has to pitch her projects to her editor at the *New York Times*. I asked Sarah how she approached pitching.

> When you pitch a story, especially as a freelancer, you start with, "I'm so and so, here's my credit, and I've worked here, here, and here. I went to school here, and I studied this and this." I'm telling you it this way because it applies to anytime you pitch yourself for a job or a contract or any type of work. "There is this thing; here's why I'm the best person to do it. Here's this amazing idea, and here are a couple of samples of my past work." That's how you pitch a story or anything. You tell your idea the way you'd tell your best friend after an awesome night out.

It's all in the telling. A great practice is to rehearse your pitch with a friend. Say it out loud. Do it a few times, so by the time you are actually pitching, you are comfortable with what you have to say and can deliver it well.

There is a dangerous trap that affects a lot of people when they are in meetings or pitching, what Mauro Porcini called "hidden rejection."

I would have all these meetings, and at first, everybody loved me. They loved me because they knew I had the support of the top leaders of the company, but I know that the moment I was heading out of the door, the vast majority of them were like, "Okay, we had fun. Back to business. That design guy is gone."

This second phase is what I call the "hidden rejection." They seem to embrace you, but in reality, they are not embracing you. This happens so many times. When I worked for 3M, one of the top executives there gave me advice that I keep close to my heart. I was telling him, "They're supporting us." But he knew they were not supporting me. He said, "They will always tell you that. They lie until they give you the money. Do not believe them, because they do have the money. If they're not giving you the money, it means that they don't really believe in you because they're using the money somewhere else."

Hidden rejection is very important to understand. There are a million ways to say no. There's one way to say yes: you fund it. That's it. The real trap in hidden rejection is keeping your own ego in check. Don't think that because they laughed at your jokes, they were charmed by you. When you leave the room, their true opinions will come out. You've got to be aware that this is not about your ego. This is about selling an idea. The only way you can sell something is if somebody pays you for it. It's really important because you can lose a tremendous amount of time and momentum by fooling yourself into thinking you were better liked or your idea was better accepted than it truly was.

Daniel Gulati told me about the mistakes people make when pitching:

I have been in several pitches where I have passed in the meeting, and the entrepreneur then pitches a completely different idea. It's the guy with the trench coat full of watches asking you to pick your favorite. VCs are looking to back entrepreneurs that have high conviction and are in it for the long haul.

It's a scary place to be when someone is throwing around shiny objects in the first meeting and hoping something sticks.

This might be a style preference, but I sometimes feel uncomfortable when the pitch seems overrehearsed or overly polished. That tends to detract from an entrepreneur's authenticity. The best pitches I have seen turn into dynamic two-way conversations pretty quickly.

People are constantly discovering new things in every product category because there is so much product available. The critical task is to get and sustain people's attention, which is essential for building brand loyalty. The most effective way to do that is to have a strong differentiator.

It is the same in every business. There are budgets to be aware of. There are limitations to be aware of. There are people that you have to get aligned with your project who can help move it forward. If you do good work, you have to do a lot of work building your foundation before you ever present an idea.

If you're designing a line of clothing, it's the same as having six hours of footage that ends up as six minutes on the air. You cut away, and you edit, you edit, you edit. That's the same thing you're doing. You're putting together a line of fashion. It's the same thing I went through with writing my play. Editing is where it all lives. In every art form it's editing. If you understand that dynamic, you're going to have a lot less trouble in aligning people with your project and knowing how to present things so you can get them through the door and get them out to the world that you want to reach.

A lot of times people go into pitches with potential financial backers, armed with a financial plan and projections. When I started my first company, people said, "How much business will you be doing in five years?" I had no idea. What I didn't realize is that neither did they.

I asked venture capitalist Daniel Gulati, when trying to obtain financing, how important is the person and their story, and how much is it just financial information? What do investors look at?

Daniel Gulati on What Investors Look For

At the early stage, you are typically focused on assessing a founding team's capabilities and insights and the attractiveness of a market that may or may not yet exist. If any financial information is available, it's likely too early to have any sort of statistical significant or predictive value, so it tends to rank lower on an investor's diligence list.

At the later stages, you do have a multiyear P&L [profit and loss], unit economics, and detailed cohort data to assess. You can observe patterns in how an executive team has actually run the business. And you can talk to real customers, suppliers, and former and current employees. At this point, the business model is set and the company is in execution mode, so that type of information is going to be much more predictive of what the company's true potential is. It's also critical for setting valuations at the later stages.

An effective narrative galvanizes investors, customers, and employees. For investors who assess hundreds of opportunities per year, a standout story will help you rise above the pack and potentially allow you to raise money on a premium valuation. If your investor's firm is a partnership, an effective story will help him or her "sell" the business to their partners.

For customers, a memorable story creates emotion, and emotion fuels customers to buy and tell their friends. That's the lifeblood of an early-stage consumer company.

Finally, the war for talent is only intensifying. Exceptional talent can go anywhere, and start-ups typically can't compete on guaranteed compensation alone. The way to attract and retain these A players is to convince them you are on a path to building something special and that they have a rare opportunity to join before it's obvious.

As the saying goes, "The money follows the stories."

What does a venture capitalist, someone who is in the position to put significant money into a business, look for as proof of concept? We know part of it is that someone is buying your product. What else is looked at?

What is most important in the beginning is evidence of customer love. In a consumer business, that's usually early-adopter customers evangelizing the mission of the company organically and referring other customers to the company, coupled with repeat usage of the product. These dynamics give VCs confidence that product-market fit exists and that the business is ready to grow by applying investment to what already works at a unit level.

In any deal, it is important to understand what the other side hopes to gain. What should entrepreneurs be aware of that investors are looking for?

Entrepreneurs need to ensure their investors are aligned on what success looks like. For a particular founder, receiving a $20 million acquisition offer might be life changing financially. But for a large venture capital fund, that is an outcome indistinguishable from $0. So the large fund may have an incentive to not sign off on the exit and push to keep the company operating independently. A simple way to assess investor alignment is to look at the size of their fund. Generally speaking, VCs will make investments hoping they can return the entire fund from the one investment. That will give you a ballpark idea of the magnitude of outcome the VC expects.

Outside of fund size, entrepreneurs should understand the value an investor provides beyond their capital, whether that be introductions, commercial opportunities, or access to specific resources. It is also critical to reference check your investors with other entrepreneurs they have worked with. When times are tough, does the investor run for the hills, or are they digging in and supporting the company?

From the entrepreneurial side, what key points should you make sure to articulate before you approach a VC or investor?

When you are pitching, less is more. It is critical to convey what you are building, why it's important, and why you'll win in the most direct way possible. Like any sales conversation, you don't want to leave it to the person on the other side of the table to try to separate the signal from the noise.

Second, VCs are not looking to fund "good enough" businesses, nor are they looking to fund categories. Their job is to identify and invest in outliers. While it is important to highlight trends and themes that are relevant to your company, you want to emphasize why you are that one bird in the flock that will fly the highest. I am fortunate to meet with hundreds of entrepreneurs every year and typically invest in three to five new companies.

Finally, you want to be the absolute best version of you. Too many entrepreneurs show up trying to emulate the Silicon Valley founder archetype du jour. More often than not, that comes across as fake. Your best strategy is to tap into your strengths and natural style.

Be who you are, not who you think you should be. You can learn from another's successful approach, but don't try to copy someone else.

Understand what an investor is looking for and be aware of what you should be looking for in an investor.

Being able to communicate your story is essential in your creative or any other type of career because that's how you attract an audience. The power of story is why James Bond has been around for sixty years, why people follow Apple's new products, and, ultimately, how you sell yourself and your business. Our brains frame information as a story. We retain that much more than we retain facts, although we always think our own stories are factual.

Look into the Stanislavski method, think about the given circumstances of what you are trying to do, and figure out your motivation for doing it. It can be a clarifying exercise and applies to all aspects of life. Answer the following first seven workbook questions using the Stanislavski method.

....

Workbook Questions

- 💡 Who are you?

- 💡 Where are you?

- 💡 When is it?

- 💡 What do you want?

- 💡 Why do you want it?

- 💡 How will you get it?

- 💡 What do you need to overcome?

- 💡 What story can you tell for a pitch about your project's origin, inspiration, fan following, or related phenomenon to increase attention and interest in your work? Or what stories and events can you engineer for such a reaction?

- 💡 What benefit does your idea bring to a potential investor or customer?

....

11

Building a Relationship with Your Customer

IN 1999 VICTORIA'S SECRET PARTNERED with Yahoo! and AOL to live-stream their fashion show for the first time. My role was to direct the show and send the video feed to them. This was before there was the bandwidth to handle full-resolution video. It was an audacious move to live-stream a show. Nothing like that had ever been done. It would be a major marketing coup, if we could pull it off. We had a meeting with the executives from all three companies to discuss how we could technically do it. The people from AOL and Yahoo! had worked together before to do what had been the largest online event to date, John Glenn's relaunch into space, with around 250,000 viewers.

"If we get a million viewers," I said, "tell the people from Victoria's Secret what's going to happen." The representatives from AOL and Yahoo! didn't respond. "The site will crash," I told them. The people from Victoria's Secret were horrified. "Is that true?" The last thing they wanted was for viewers to be unable to watch the show because of a server issue. But I saw it differently. "This is great," I told them. "It's like a concert being sold out. Everybody will want to get in. People will want to see what all the excitement is about. You can't buy that kind of press." Over a million and a half people tried to watch, and the servers crashed, driving up demand for the show. We archived it online so viewers could watch it later. It ended up being a huge win for Victoria's Secret because it got what they hoped for—people's attention. Stories ran in television, online, and in print with the headline "Victoria's Secret Crashes the Internet." The servers crashing didn't get attention; the *story* that the online show was so popular that it crashed the servers did. It was a major marketing coup thanks to the story that was told.

This situation strengthened my relationship with Victoria's Secret. They saw that I was as concerned with the success of this event as they were. The story also created great consumer interest about the brand, which was not that well known at the time.

All marketing is storytelling, and marketing is about creating a relationship with your customer. So how do you do that? How do you identify your market, get to know them, and communicate in the most effective way? Online shopping has created different problems for business and new strategies for establishing ongoing customer relationships.

Amy Smilovic, founder and CEO of the women's fashion line Tibi, stays in touch with her customers and uses her own gut instincts to know what will or won't work.

> At our size, I don't have to be everything to everyone. So if myself and my design team, if we make up this nucleus of an idea of what we want to wear, I don't know if it's what you want to wear, but I know that someone will want to wear it if we do. If it doesn't do well, it just means that somehow I got the pricing wrong and I didn't communicate well enough in a marketing perspective, because if I want to wear this coat, can I find five hundred people in this entire world that want to wear it? Yeah, if the marketing is good, I can find them. If my social media person over there is doing her job, she can find them on Instagram. And so that's a great thing. I don't have to worry anymore about a store's ability to tell

the story. You can have this conversation directly with the customer. If you love it, you're not wrong. When we've made bad decisions, it's always been because we didn't love it first.

Online retail has had a massive effect on brick-and-mortar retail. Social media isn't social; it's media, paid media. Although the technology is new, the business model is old. It's like radio and television: they give you the content, ostensibly for free, but they sell your data for marketing and advertising. Facebook isn't a tech company; it's a marketing company. So is Instagram. So is Twitter. So is Snapchat. So is Pinterest. So is LinkedIn. So are Google and YouTube.

A book I read back in junior high school had a big effect on me, *The Hidden Persuaders* by Vance Packard. It was first published in 1957 and was incredibly prescient. It was the first book to study motivational research and apply it to marketing, advertising, and political campaigns. Companies such as Kellogg's and Post cereals would put their colorful boxes at eye level for kids, so they'd grab the boxes. Shopping was never the same for me after reading that book.

In the same way, when I met Ryan Urban, founder of BounceX, I was fascinated that he took behavioral economics and applied it to online shopping. It's just as important to establish relationships with your customers online as it is with a store if you want them to come back. I asked Ryan what he thought of customer service surveys and how they relate to the online consumer. He told me:

> I don't believe in surveys because if you ask someone a question like, "Why are you interested in buying this product?" They don't know what the actual answer is. "Why do you buy from this site?" They don't know the psychology behind why. The key is observing people's behavior.
>
> I never took psychology classes, but I was always fascinated by it. I'd watch infomercials, and there was one for a paint

sprayer. I hate manual labor. I watched this infomercial, and I wanted to paint my house. I hate work. What was it that made me want to buy this thing?

The first [business] book I ever read was on infomercials and the thought process behind them. It was about behavioral psychology, observing people, then figuring out how to influence them. How do you think about things from someone else's perspective? That's really it.

When you walk into a store, how annoying is it when someone comes up to you right away and asks, "How can I help you?" I haven't even looked at anything yet! After I look at a bunch of things, if someone comes over and says, "Would you like to see if I have it in your size?" that's okay. How do you think about things from the person on your website's perspective? That was the problem with all big e-commerce companies. They think of people as numbers because that's what their analytics says. They don't realize that it's an actual person, on the other side on their website, doing stuff.

How often do you go to a website and say, "I want to sign up for email"? Never. But if you're going to want me to sign up for your email, what's in it for me, and when's the right time to ask? It turns out if you wait so they look at products, and then you ask them, "I know you're not buying this now, but when you're thinking of buying this, would you like to get 15 percent off?" Then you say, "Okay, cool. Why don't you put in your email, and I'll give you this code and send some other relevant stuff to you?" People will respond to that. There are humans on your website. What's in it for them? That's the psychology behind it.

We had to figure out, what are your cues? Online we could figure out what someone likes or not. If the product goes on sale, let the person know. People love getting price-cut emails. Create purely relevant marketing. But you have to pay attention to what people actually like and what they don't like. If someone looked at a product page for five seconds, they don't care if it went on sale—they don't want it.

That means you start with the customer service, not the technology. Focus on the client and address their needs.

THE CONSUMER'S MIND-SET

There is an abundance of product to choose from in every category, from food, fashion, and electronics to movies and news. Are we rational? Do we make decisions for good reasons? How do people decide what to buy and when to buy? Cognitive neuroscientist Moran Cerf looked into how consumers make judgments and decisions.

He told me that buying a bottle of wine is something most of us can relate to and involves deciding about something most of us know little about. When you go into a wine store, you'll notice the prices go from the cheapest to the most expensive in each category. Most often, people pick the one in the middle. If the wine seller wants to sell a more expensive wine, they up the price on either end of the lineup, which ups the midrange price, and people spend more. If you ask, "Why did you buy this wine?" the customer will usually say, "I don't know too much about wine, so I bought the middle one." But they didn't decide what the range is; the seller decided for them. They shift the perceptions by shifting the prices. The brain is biased all the time. We don't control the biases. We think we know how things work, but we don't.

Moran explained a concept in neuroscience called the "Pain of Paying," which is showing that when people pay, they actually feel a bit of pain. The centers in the brain called the insula, the part of the brain that actually makes you feel pain, is active when you pay. It is proportional, to some extent, to the amount of money that you would spend. And it even changes by how you pay. What do you think is more painful, cash or credit?

Cash is more painful because you actually see your money moving from you to someone else. Credit cards are less painful because you receive the bill once a month. That's why credit card debt is such a problem. As so many transactions have moved online, more and more money is spent without the pain of spending cash. Debt increases as we move further away from actual money. That is why Las Vegas casinos use chips. It removes the pain of losing your money—until you cash in your chips.

Whether it's what Ryan Urban is doing at BounceX or what Moran as a neuroscientist is studying, they are both trying to change our focus from just explaining how the brain works to actually seeing how it works in environments that are very complex—such as purchasing, decision making, and marketing—and understanding why things work the way they do.

It makes no logical sense for people to line up around the block to buy Apple products that none of them needs. They all have functioning mobile phones, but they want the new products. Consumerism is driven by creating desire. These aren't products that are going to keep you alive; these are the products that you want. Telling a story that relates to the dreams and aspirations that you have is always a more effective sell.

Ralph Lauren wanted to dress like Cary Grant or Gary Cooper did in the movies. He couldn't find clothes like that in the stores. He built a global fashion and lifestyle brand by selling those Hollywood dreams. I asked Ralph how he was able to so successfully tap into the psyche of his customer. He told me, "I know what the consumer wants because I am the consumer."

I asked Tim Ferriss, best-selling author of *The 4-Hour Workweek*, how he knew there was a market for a book about lifestyle design.

I didn't know there was a market for my writing or for some of the start-ups that I ended up being involved with like Uber, Evernote, or Twitter. I perhaps naively assumed that if I scratch my own itch and create something that I couldn't find for myself, other people will want it. When I wrote *The 4-Hour Workweek*, I was twenty-nine or thirty years old. There were probably many people in my demographic who went to the bookstore to try to find something about lifestyle design, making a lot of money, but not letting it control your life, and how to design a career that services that. I couldn't find it.

I ended up doing research and then writing the book. I assumed that if that void was something I sought to fill, other people might feel the same way. It was an educated guess.

Publishers have to believe a book will sell before they are willing to buy it. They don't like to take chances. What was your pitch? What was the compelling reason publishers thought, "Okay, we'll buy this"?

Tim was turned down by twenty-seven publishers. He persevered. Finally, Crown Publishing, a division of Random House, bought the book. I asked him why he thinks they went for it. He said he convinced them he could sell the book:

> If you look at how I have competed, if you look at how I've won National Championship of Kickboxing, if you look at A, B, C, D, and E, I am all in. I will do anything required. If you're not going to bet on the concept, bet on me. I think that's why they took the gamble.

The gamble paid off. Tim's book was on the *New York Times* best-seller list for four years, was translated into thirty-five languages, sold 1.3 million copies, and launched Tim's career. His initial insight, like Ralph Lauren's, was simple: if I'm looking for something like this, so are others.

A successful business, as Kathy Ireland explained,

> is knowing who you are serving and who your customers are. It can be difficult when you are creative and have something that you've just poured your heart and soul into. Knowing who

you're serving, what their budget is, is critical if you're going to make a business out of it. Listening is really important. That's how we started our brand many years ago, by listening to our customer.

Art is a business. Books and movies have created a mystique around the artist that bears little resemblance to the real world. There is no intrinsic value in art. It is all based on what the buyer thinks it is worth. As an artist gets purchased by a prominent collector or gallery, that ups the price. That is also marketing, which sets up others to buy it who see it as not only something they might love, but a wise investment as well.

I asked painter Zaria Forman what she thinks is the main misconception the public has about artists:

> The business side of art is half the battle! No one tells you that in art school, or at least they didn't tell me. And honestly, I don't think most artists are very good at the business side— I know I'm not!
>
> Marketing is a huge part of this. Social media is an important tool that artists have today to market themselves without spending any money. I find that consistency is key. Create a clear vision of what your work is about, what you want to say with it, and share some form of that in everything you put out. In advertising they call it branding!

Not every business owner dreams of becoming a huge global enterprise. You can live quite well with a much smaller company that is well run and profitable. However, that, too, requires smart marketing.

What is the most effective medium for marketing? Joe Polish has a new, old approach:

There are three things you need to sell:

1. A product or service
2. A sales pitch or a marketing method
3. A delivery system, which could be social media, email, TV, radio, face-to-face selling, whatever

My favorite form of marketing is direct mail, and the reason is there's so much noise in the electronic boxes and there's no noise in the mailbox. There's such an opportunity with direct mail because the problem with looking at a whole list of emails or messages or whatever is that you're looking at thousands of different decisions calling out for your attention. But when someone gets a card, when someone gets a book, when someone gets a package, it totally differentiates you, and it will be a thousand times more impactful to get the same message written on a card than if it was by email.

CREATE AN EXPERIENCE

Know what you're selling. Sounds simple. It isn't. A lot of businesses don't realize what they are selling. Polaroid was an iconic brand, synonymous with instant (which initially took one minute) pictures. They thought they were selling proprietary cameras and film. They weren't. They were selling instant gratification. You didn't have to send your film off for developing and wait; you got to share the picture right away. When digital photography was developed, no company was better positioned than Polaroid to take advantage of the technological shift to digital, instant, photography. They didn't. They didn't realize what business they were in. Digital image capture disrupted the film business. Polaroid went bankrupt.

Whenever you pass an Apple store, wherever you are in the world, it's busy. It shows you that brick and mortar is a viable way to sell goods. Their retail presentation is consistent with the brand image of hip innovation. Retail is ripe for disruption.

We constantly hear the term *disruption* in terms of businesses that move into a space and create a new product or new way of doing things. Uber disrupted the private transportation business, Airbnb disrupted the hospitality business, and Away disrupted the luggage business. One of the first investors of Away was Daniel Gulati, who told me:

> *Disruption* is an overused term these days. To me, it describes a very specific process where small start-ups launch new products at the bottom end of a market, attract customers, and move upmarket to upend established competitors.
>
> Away luggage launched by solving a problem that the founders themselves had—finding awesome luggage they were proud of at a reasonable price. Since then, they have executed on a much broader vision of improving the overall travel experience. Travel products like luggage are a piece of that vision, but it's very much a starting point. I still feel like Away is in the early innings of what they could achieve. Their success to date has largely been a function of creating a truly inspiring brand, attention to detail on both the physical product and the experience layer around the product, and laying a strong financial foundation for the business to succeed in the future.

I asked Daniel what attracted him to Away and why he invested in it:

Two things stood out about the Away founders. First, both were senior employees at Warby Parker, a direct to consumer brand that scaled quickly off impressive fundamentals. They had seen the playbook on how to go from zero to a very large business and learned specifics on how to set up supply chains and build a loved brand on social media.

Second, both were very focused on the details of the physical product. In our first meeting, we spent twenty minutes or so discussing why the wheels on Away suitcases were superior, all the way down to the company's sourcing strategy and the physics of why those particular wheels led to a smooth ride on almost any surface. Even though we invested prior to the product being finalized, I got comfortable pretty quickly that whatever product they were going to put out into the world would be very well thought out and executed.

Dylan Lauren created an experience that makes people want to buy a lot of candy. It's colorful, fun, and nostalgic for parents who see some of the classic candy brands. It's a hard experience to replicate online. Dylan is not only selling candy but also selling fun:

I am not a tech-savvy person at all, and I rarely shop online. Especially with fashion, I like to touch things and try them on. I want to know exactly what it looks like and how it fits. This is an interesting debate because I don't want to be on a computer all day. I want to see the store. I think people tend to buy more if they're actually in the environment. However, there are people who are lazy or they don't live by a store or they like the convenience of getting shipped to them. So I think there are several types of people, and there are people who do both. I would be shocked if brick and mortar went out. A store is the place to tell the story. I think that it's very important, however, to have a good online presence. I'm working on that, although that's not my passion. I find it a little frustrating, to be honest, to have people who are experiencing my store that way. My passion is the in-store experience. That's why I'm trying to open more stores, catch up with them.

People buy an emotional connection. It's not about a particular product. Ralph Lauren isn't selling clothes. He is selling status and good taste.

The Ralph Lauren mansion on Seventy-Second and Madison is an experience. When you go in there to buy, it's like you're wandering around some rich person's mansion who left all their beautiful things out for you to look at, including the artwork on the wall. It doesn't look like any other store. It's the experience that people go there for. When Ralph opened a store in Moscow, the first thing they sold were five Ricky crocodile handbags for $25,000 each. This is a purse to carry your stuff around in. Why do people spend $25,000 on a handbag?

To some, it's aspirational. People want the best—or what they perceive is the best. Some people feel good only if they spend a lot of money on something, especially if other people know it.

Ralph believes, from a business point of view, that you have to start at the top. If he started with a $250 purse, although he could do a lot of business, that's the price range where he would end up. If he starts at the top, even if he sells very few bags at the $25,000 price point, once he's established at that level, he can then sell to the masses and build an even bigger business.

While in Vietnam, Joe Polish went to a Louis Vuitton store and saw a purse for $4,000. Next door was a knockoff store that had all the same styles for much less. The $4,000 purse was $60:

I looked at the $60 purse and went back to the Louis Vuitton store, and it looked identical. I mean identical, but the weirdest thing was, there were people in the Louis Vuitton store and there were people in the knockoff store. Two different sets of humans buying a different thing. Are they buying aspiration?

Are they buying status? What people are buying is a feeling, what it makes them feel like.

The empathetic response, knowing how your customer feels, allows you to relate to them, knowing who they are and what they're going to respond to. If you understand desire, you understand what selling is all about, which goes beyond the product to a message or philosophy. Tom Bilyeu explains:

> We're selling empowerment at the end of the day, and being able to take control of your body is the first step to living a life that you can come to with the full weight of your personality and desires. Then the other is the mind and getting people into a virtuous cycle. It's a false dichotomy that the mind, the brain specifically, is separate from the body. They are interconnected, and I don't mean that in a woo-woo spiritual way. Literally, there are neurons in your digestive tract; there are neurons in your brain that communicate back and forth.
>
> Once people realize that the real journey is to engage with your life as fully and completely as possible to accomplish whatever you want to do, you need to take care of your body; you need to take care of your mind. What you eat is so critically important that that seemed like the opening salvo to us, but we're looking deeply at other things.
>
> For a brand to succeed today, you've got be more than just a product. You need to solve problems and add value to your customer at every touch point. Even your marketing should be intrinsically value added. Take my podcast, *Impact Theory*, which is shot like a TV show. I've had countless people tell me that it's changed their lives. But ultimately the show is as much a marketing vehicle as it is an end product.

Connection and Community

Creating community is the goal of a lot of companies. It builds brand loyalty, which is very good for business. Communities get together and share common interests and goals. Harley-Davidson creates a community of people who love motorcycle riding, on Harleys, of course.

Creating communities online, which is also great for business, is much harder to do. Amanda Hesser and Merrill Stubbs discovered the power of a community with the common interest of a lifestyle around cooking that has helped them build their business. Investors look for community because the strength and allure of the community can lead to exponential growth. As Daniel Gulati has observed:

User communities are most powerful when they are empowered— when companies actually leverage input from customers to make their products and businesses better. This motivates customers to interact further, creating a flywheel of deeper community engagement driving superior product execution.

I asked Daniel, how do you know when you're putting together a business who your potential market is, and how do you present that?

For markets that exist today, it's important to narrow in on the subset of the market that is actually addressable by your company. Another common mistake is to simply assume you will gain a small percentage of a large market. This top-down can be useful as a sanity check, but you should be building your market sizing bottom-up.

For markets that don't yet exist, founders should lay out the "need to believe" around why a large market will exist in the future. It can also be helpful to lay out proxies—clues or facts that point to a large potential opportunity.

It is important to know not only who your customer really is, but also how to get in front of them. Daymond John started FUBU before the days of e-commerce but during the days of the growth of hip hop culture. He did fieldwork.

At that time, hip hop was purely music, but had a way to walk, talk, and dress. Every dollar I had, I would buy whatever the rappers were wearing: Le Coq Sportif, Alessi, Fila, and Timberland.

But Timberland came out with a comment that said, "We don't sell our boots to drug dealers." That was in the newspaper. We were frustrated because if you live in New York, the guys definitely in the streets of Brooklyn, Queens, and the Bronx wore Timberlands with everything all year-round. They would wear Timberlands with Speedos, if they had to. Rappers were feeling frustrated with the way that corporations were speaking to them.

I got frustrated and said to myself, "Well, nobody is going to really support and value the customers that love them no matter what the color was." I came out with FUBU, For Us By Us, in 1989. Many people thought that FUBU was only for African Americans, but I would be just as prejudiced if I made it only for African Americans. It really was for everybody who loved this culture. I made forty of these hats. I remember looking all over uptown Manhattan for a hat. I could not find it. I knew where the guys hung out and sold the hats out of the trunk of my car.

I knew everything about consumers because I was one of my consumers. I knew their ages, what they listened to. They liked large, but they didn't like extra-large. They liked blue, red, whatever the case was. I knew every single thing about them.

It's about knowing who your customers are. Daymond quoted Mary Kay, who owned her namesake Fortune 500 cosmetics company: "Everyone has an invisible sign hanging from their neck saying, 'Make me feel important.' Never forget this message when working with people."

Leandra Medine has been very successful at attracting an audience and building a community based on her editorial approach of Man Repeller. She has a strong point of view, which is essential for any publication, and a clear idea of how she wants to engage her readers:

> I had this idea of how the media business should be run and how intimate it should feel. I always wanted our users to feel like, when they were logging into Man Repeller, they were getting on the phone with one of their closest friends and feeling like, "I don't know what you're going to say to me today and I might not actually care about the topic, but I know that the way you deliver this information is always so compelling to me, so I'm just going to listen, and then I'm going to hang up and I'm going to think about it and I'm going to come back tomorrow." It's as simple as that.
>
> Man Repeller's core competency is to connect to other women, make them feel more understood and less alone. We are a community first and foremost, and part of what makes a community feel connected is having some skin in the game. You read a story and you're invited on this emotional roller coaster with its writer and you have a visceral response to it.
>
> When people asked me who the most important audience member of Man Repeller is, it's always a woman who's in her formative years, who's learning how to speak to herself, because so much of the way that we talk to ourselves is commanded by social currency, and when you're living on the Internet and the ways in which you are being told to be don't actually serve you.

When I was researching Sally Singer, creative director at *Vogue*, I read a quote of hers that I found interesting: "Emotion: it's actually the glue that cements a reader's allegiance to us." When I interviewed Sally, I asked her to explain what she meant by that and how it related to storytelling in *Vogue* magazine: "Our strongest engagement is when people feel moved by things. If we don't tell emotional stories, we're not telling anything."

Roy Wood Jr. doesn't communicate with his audience only when he is on *The Daily Show* or performing in a club. He is constantly in touch by using social media. Roy believes constant communication is essential. It not only creates a bond with his fans but is also a great way to market himself and keep them aware of upcoming performances:

> How do I communicate with my audience? Whatever communication they use. I'm on most social media. It's about having a presence on multiple platforms. It's definitely about being anywhere those people are. And sometimes engaging people that look like they would be fans of what you do.
>
> Twitter is about conversation. Instagram is about pictures. Facebook is about elongated opinions. So you figure out how to present your brand to each platform, and then that will beget the engagement.

Chef Hillary Sterling knows how important not only the food but also the customer experience is when you walk into her restaurant, Vic's New York:

> It starts once you walk in the door. This isn't just all about me, I might be the person that gets you back there, but there's a handful of people that without them I can't be successful. It's the person that greets you, the host, it's the manager, it's the bartender, it's the server, it's even the food runner, and then it comes down to me.

If any of those people aren't falling into place, then your experience is going to be altered. So I need all of those people to say good evening to you when you walk in the door and to say good-bye to you when you leave because the most important thing is saying good-bye to a guest.

There's a restaurant in the West Village I walk into, and they ask, "Would you like a Negroni? Nice to see you." I don't know if I want a Negroni, but I'm going to have a Negroni because they asked me if I wanted it. That place is so expensive and so delicious, but you know what, I will go back there over and over again and probably have that Negroni every time because they ask and they remember. It's really what it comes down to. The food, superfluous—it's about the service.

It's no different in a restaurant than a retail store or an office. It's all the same thing. How do you make people feel welcome, and how do you make them want to come back? The important lesson is what Hillary said: "My job is to make them happy." That's true when you're selling anything. You want people to feel good so they come back again. Whether they're buying the clothing you're designing, whether they're buying the food that you're selling, or whether you're their accountant and you've done a good job, it's about making the customer happy.

Workbook Questions

- 💡 Who is your customer?

- 💡 Where do they look for information or shop?

- 💡 What is your "avatar," and what do they aspire to and desire?

- 💡 How can you best communicate with them?

- 💡 How can you make someone feel welcome?

- 💡 How can you make an emotional connection with your customer?

12

How to Build a Brand

BEING A "BRAND" HAS BECOME the necessary descriptive term when referring to a product or service, be it fashion, computers, movies, cars, mobile phones, or celebrities. But before you can create a brand, you must understand what a brand is. It is imperative to remember that it all starts with the product or service, which is the foundation that brands are built on. The strategies and protocols of creating a brand are the same no matter what the product or service.

What Is a Brand?

A brand is a mission. It stands for something. It makes you feel a certain way when you see it. It makes you feel a certain way about yourself when you use that product. It gives you something to connect to.

—RANDI ZUCKERBERG

A brand is how a company makes you feel, based on what their product does for you. The stronger the feeling, the more valuable the brand.

—DANIEL GULATI

A brand is a collection of values attached to a word or an image.
—**VANESSA FRIEDMAN**

It's an imaginary space that stands for some idea or feeling. When you look at any brand, you know what they are. It's a curated imaginary space that emits ideas or dreams.
—**BRANDON MAXWELL**

A brand is how I feel about something. It is how I identify myself.
—**LAURA EDWARDS**

A brand is an entity that has something to sell, usually from it, or that defines something that has a commercial value.
—**SALLY SINGER**

Brands are an interesting combination of design and symbolism that defines the visual landscape of our popular culture, on apparel, embedded in media and events, and on buildings—think of the golden arches of McDonald's or the Apple logo with no words on their stores. What is Nike's slogan? You know it without my telling you ("Just do it"). Another way to understand a slogan is that it's the moral of the story.

Brands are intangible assets of tremendous value because they gain our attention, enabling good brands to create relationships with consumers. People who have relationships with a brand buy their products, whether they are fashion, phones, movies, or financial services.

What makes establishing that relationship—some call it "a dialogue"—with the consumer so difficult is the incredible number of choices available to us that are constantly competing for our attention. In most cases, there is plenty of supply; what's important is creating demand, and the only way that happens is by attracting and retaining the attention of the consumer.

WHAT'S YOUR BRAND STORY?

The most precious commodity out there is our attention. How do you get it, and how do you keep it, so you can attract customers? An ongoing brand story is essential to accomplishing that.

"A picture is worth a thousand words" refers to the notion that a complex idea can be conveyed with just a single image. In creating a strong brand, that image is the logo.

The crucifix is a logo, as are all religious symbols. The tenets of religion are the same as the beliefs that create a brand, a story that compels one to believe in the unique benefits of whatever it is. Just like the crucifix, the apple, the polo pony, the swoosh, or Mickey Mouse, the logo communicates without words.

Christianity comes with a compelling narrative that has lasted more than two thousand years. The crucifix is one of the most powerful symbols in the world and exemplifies what a brand is:

1. There is immediate recognition.
2. A brand has to stand for something.
3. It is reinforced by long-term consistency.
4. There is loyalty to the symbol.

The strongest brands have their missionaries—or brand ambassadors, people who sing its praises—just like the believers in Apple do today. Like some ancient religious ritual, thousands of people line up at Apple stores around the world to buy the newest iPhone. No company has brand evangelists like Apple.

A brand is a story well told. A compelling narrative is the essential characteristic of any successful brand. However, no matter how talented or creative you may be, creating a brand is difficult because it requires getting and holding on to people's attention. It also takes time. We live in a constant hailstorm of data and images, and to get people's attention, an ongoing brand story is critical. That story needs to use emotion and anticipation to communicate the core values you're trying to sell, values that you know resonate with your consumer base.

Storytelling is essential. Marketing is storytelling. When it's good, it's a compelling story. When it's a list of features and benefits, it's not a story. It's boring; most people don't remember facts and figures. Apple, Nike, and BMW never advertise their product features and benefits. They tell a seductive story, sometimes just visually.

Tom Bilyeu: Brand Is a Relationship

A brand is a living, breathing entity that acts much like how the brain and body communicate with each other. The company and the users of their products communicate in this completely symbiotic way, where they're feeling like each other's happinesses, discontents, frustrations, pains, and they each respond accordingly.

When as a brand you give something that the community believes is incredibly valuable, they go to bat for you, man, and they'll tell anybody who will listen. On the flip side, if you do something that they feel is not in line with what the brand stands for, they'll let you know that. As long as you listen to your customers and respond in a transparent way, they will stay with you even through reasonable missteps.

It becomes this dance of communication, where if you get it right, it is incredible. We're living in a time where I actually have relationships over social media with some of the people that we've impacted. People that have lost a hundred pounds, people that have a Quest-themed wedding. It's crazy. Being able to feel really connected with those people is unreal, and the feedback that they give us is the same. That they've penetrated that corporate veil, and they see real people, that means a lot.

Narrative is incredibly important to a brand. In fact, it is critical to a brand. It might not be critical to a product, but it's critical to a brand. If a brand wants to transcend its products and create a lifestyle, they have to get into narrative. Why is narrative so important? Because humans are wired for it, and that's how we transmit complicated ideas.

There is an important difference between a brand and branding. Branding is how you communicate your brand message via public relations, marketing, and advertising, essentially anytime you are communicating about the brand. However, you can't do branding without a clear brand identity, which is the most valuable equity that any company has.

When Walt Disney was building the Disney brand, he asked himself, "What would Mickey do?" as a barometer for whether something was "on brand." Ralph Lauren has done the same thing. His brand stands for status and good taste, and his own desires have served as his brand barometer. Before Ralph went public, it wasn't the clothes that gave his company such a high valuation; it was the brand equity he'd built on a global scale. Creating his brand took years of consistent messaging and reinforcement through all the ways the brand was communicated to consumers, from the marketing and advertising to the in-store experience.

When I was with Ralph, sorting through all of the images for editing into his lifetime achievement award, I paused to take in all these pictures of him on horseback looking like he was in a cowboy movie, driving an incredible vintage Bugatti, outside a beautiful mansion. I said to him, "That guy looks pretty cool," and he said, "Yeah, I wish I was that guy." That was his public image, his aspirational lifestyle. The brand was the story created around that. Ralph's image and the Polo brand became one.

With entrepreneurs, there is often no dividing line between what the business is and who they are as an individual. Their company is a vehicle for personal expression.

Tim Ferriss is a best-selling author, does speaking engagements, had a television show, wrote a highly viewed blog, and has a very popular podcast, all based on who he is. He is the product, the embodiment, of the Tim Ferriss brand. Like every public personality, Tim gets a lot of negative comments. I asked Tim how he protects himself from the rigors of being famous and the inevitable toxic responses he gets online.

> I view being part of the product, a face associated with my books, is a price I pay for getting what I hope to teach to the greatest number of people possible. I don't view myself as famous compared to any real celebrities, but I don't try to create a separate persona because I think that, especially in a digital age where you have so many different touch points, people can eventually gather enough data that they'll be able to figure out, "That was total BS."
>
> I try to be as straightforward as possible. It ensures that the fans I tracked are the fans that I want. I will actively call my herd and try to push away fans that I don't think are congruent with my sense of humor. On my blog, if I'm getting too concerned about what other people think or I'm dialing back on, let's say, dropping F bombs. I enjoy that. I like using artfully implemented profanity. I'll try to post with a bunch of curse words. Some people get offended, and then they'll leave. I don't really focus on what a lot of people seem to focus on these days, which is building a personal brand. I'm not interested.

A personal brand used to be the domain of movie stars, politicians, entertainers, and athletes. Now it has become a strategy used by many to build their careers.

For example, Karlie Kloss has been strategic about staying relevant without overexposing herself. "This industry is very competitive," she says. "You have to be able to adapt to change, transform, and keep up." She has certainly done this in her career. When she cut her long hair into a bob, it was a risky move for a highly in-demand model who was known for a particular look. But rather than staying complacent, Karlie adapted by changing her hair, altering her "product." It was a risk that paid off. *Vogue* declared her new bob "the cut of the moment" in a four-page spread and dubbed it "the Karlie." That *Vogue* article took a simple haircut and turned it into a story that transformed Karlie's career.

She has used her success from modeling to build a solid brand and is parlaying it into other businesses, such as designing jeans, "Karlie's Kookies," and "Kode with Klossy," to teach coding to empower young women ages thirteen to eighteen.

All the decisions that I've made in my career, including representation and management, which is a big part of the success of the career, I've made those decisions because of business reasons.

I want to inspire other young women across the country to follow their dreams, to feel good in their own skin.

Well executed, good stories can help sell a product, create an ad campaign, define a brand, or change a career. Karlie's story is about empowering young women through health and education. Leandra Medine's highest calling, through Man Repeller, is to connect women to one another through the art of storytelling.

There is an overabundance of product in every category. What separates products that are commodities from those that are perceived as special is the brand story. That's the primary differentiator. If people don't relate to the brand, the product is just another thing. Story is what attracts the most precious commodity out there—our attention—and in order to create a brand, attention must be paid.

When it comes to creating a brand, I asked Simon Sinek if people invest in another person's passion or another person's product. Simon told me that was the wrong question:

> Because it conflates two things that those things would be mutually exclusive, and sometimes they are, and when they are, it's a transaction. If I need a toothbrush, I don't care which— I just want a toothbrush. That's a transactional thing. I'm buying a product.
>
> But if somebody has a passion for a new way of looking at toothbrushes and shares their passion in their marketing with us about why they made this toothbrush, then we find ourselves being drawn not to the toothbrush, but to the story behind that toothbrush.
>
> There are products that people are passionate for in the same category that people don't have passion for a product. People are passionate for their Apple computers, but nobody's really passionate for their Dell, yet they basically do the same things. One is a transaction. I need a computer. The other one is I need that computer. There's many things like that. If there's a compelling story that we can personally relate to, I buy the passion. If there isn't, I buy the product.

COMPELLING STORYTELLING

Feeling a part of something is a hugely important factor for a brand to be successful. People who buy Apple products and certain fashion brands all have unifying beliefs and symbols that identify and hold them together.

Tom Bilyeu knows how critical narrative is to a brand:

Narrative is incredibly important to a brand. It might not be critical to a product, but it's critical to a brand. So if a brand wants to transcend its products and create a lifestyle, they've got to get into narrative. Why is narrative so important? Because humans are wired for it, and that's how we transmit complicated ideas. Humans can bond over things that we tell via narrative. "This is my God." Now we're instantly connected over that, and that all happens through narrative.

Ben Parr researched something he calls the parasocial relationship:

[It's] where we build this two-way relationship when we feel a relationship with brands and celebrities and figures. Many people could probably tell me what they believe are the personality traits of a Taylor Swift, Lady Gaga, Sheryl Sandberg, or whomever you admire or think about. We really don't know. Most of us don't know these people in real life. We don't know their actual personality, but we feel very strong relationships with them, just like we can feel very strong relationships with fictional characters in *Game of Thrones*, for example. In a lot of cases, people could feel stronger relationships and feelings for these figures than they do with their own families. I had a friend who worked for a major celebrity who came out in favor of Obamacare, and this celebrity's Facebook wall was suddenly filled with a whole bunch of people saying, "I thought I knew you. How dare you? I can't believe you'd betray me like this."

Dylan Lauren
on Designing a World

Dylan Lauren, founder of Dylan's Candy Bar, had stories running through her head when she was conceptualizing her business. She knew she wanted to create an immersive environment that encouraged shopping. Her favorite movie when she was a kid was, as you might guess, *Willy Wonka and the Chocolate Factory*. She loves Willy Wonka.

I also loved Disney and Alice in Wonderland, The Wizard of Oz, *and all those fantasy movies. For me it was about the whimsical set design. I always felt like it would be fun to shop in a world like an actual Candy Land. I wanted to create that because I had seen that FAO Schwartz was doing it with toys and Niketown was doing it with athletic wear. But there was no candy store that made you feel like you were in an environment. I love candy, and I don't want to go to World of Nuts or whatever. I wanted a real fun environment.*

As an artist I was very heavily involved in the actual design of all the fixtures, trying to replicate how to make a Starlight mint into a stool and how to make it more fun to sit at a bar than just sitting on a stool. I also knew subconsciously that's what helps attract people and make it a destination, versus just another candy store. I think having been inspired by my dad [Ralph Lauren], knowing it's a competitive market, I wanted to create the best candy store.

We attract people here of all ages. Our actual target market and what I set out to do was to make it a store for adults and a kid in the adult, which is what Disney does. I don't like when people say, "Oh, it's a cute gift store." You're actually my target group because everyone loves candy and wants to feel young at heart. The colors make you feel that way. We play music and have over two hundred candy songs from every genre. So older people are like, "Oh my god, I remember 'Lollipop Guild,'" and other people know the new hip hop songs. Downstairs there's also classic vintage candy brands that were around when I was growing up. So when parents come in with their kids, they see those candies, too, and the nostalgia that it triggers is very effective.

It's a full environment that gets you in the mood to want to be shopping. Our mission is to ignite the inner child and creative spirit in everyone and to merge pop art, fashion, and pop culture with the candy.

What Dylan has created is a brand story you can walk through. There is a phenomenal attention to detail, and that's the distinguishing difference. It's not good enough to do a colorful tabletop; it's a mosaic of colorful gumballs, and the legs are peppermint sticks. Every bit of detail is thought out, and that's so important in terms of creating a clear brand story. It doesn't just happen. It takes a lot of work.

A compelling narrative is essential for creating a brand. Product alone isn't enough. The story is what emotionally connects us to it. The term *authenticity* is used a lot. I asked Stephanie Jones if a brand story needs to be authentic to work. Or does it just need to be a good story that gets peopled invested emotionally?

There's actually a human behind that product. There's a soul, and that is the brand ethos of the product. That's what it's built upon.

If you want to have longevity with your brand, you have to have authenticity. I think that's at the root of everything. A lot of brands can have great press and have great product placement, but if they're not emotionally connecting with the consumer, I don't know what their longevity will be because you have to authentically connect with the consumer in order to build that brand loyalty.

Nisolo, one of our consumer brands, is a sustainable fashion and accessories line for men and women. Not only are they a leading sustainable fashion brand in the industry, but they put their Peruvian factory workers' children through the education system from grade school to college. They are just a really good company with good humans who cofounded it.

As a consumer, if you can buy a pair of shoes, or a tote, from a brand that's actually making a difference in human lives, specifically these children, why wouldn't you buy from them instead of buying from someone else? It's a great product, but knowing the heart of that company is equally important. That's one of the touch points you need to know to resonate with the consumer. That's the authenticity and story behind Nisolo. The brand's founding principles, mission, and commitment to hand-crafted, ethically made products are what we worked to high-light in a meaningful way. By combining a quality product with authenticity, and storytelling, you're able to emotionally con-nect to a consumer, and there's a lot of value added there.

It's important to remember that first and foremost, the prod-uct has to be desirable. Despite all the wonderful things a com-pany may do, people won't buy the product if it doesn't appeal to them, no matter what the company is doing socially.

Debbie Millman has worked in graphic design and branding for thirty years. In 2009 she cofounded the world's first mas-ter's program in branding at the School of Visual Arts in New York City. When Debbie was president of Sterling Brands, one of the world's leading brand consultancies, she worked on the logo and brand identity for Burger King, Hershey's, Häagen-Dazs (fun fact: it's Debbie's actual handwriting on the packaging), Tropi-cana, *Star Wars*, Gillette, Pepsi, and the No More movement. In 2005 she started one of the first podcasts, called *Design Matters*, which is still going strong. Debbie has authored six books on branding and design.

Forget innovation and think about brand building. There is no time anymore to go to an agency to commission research, gather results of the research after a few months, and then act on that. That business model for those agencies is death, for the companies is death. It is not the time anymore where you go again to an agency who will build your campaign for the year and then you have the TV campaign. There is still space for TV, but the reality is you need to keep creating content continu-ously day by day. Understanding how people talk and behave. By the way, that same amount of money that you needed to build that TV campaign you still need to have.

Design is not just the packaging of Pepsi or Lays. That's designing in brand building. It's what I call Branding 2.0. In the past, the most important piece of content for a company like PepsiCo was the TV ad. Anything else was supporting the TV ad. Then you will go to a store to buy the Pepsi, eventually you had the promotion to link back to the TV ad, but most of the time it was just the transaction. I get what I want to refresh myself. Today you go to a store, if there is a special edition of Pepsi that we did or if there is a special flavor of Pepsi that was created with a famous chef, or if there is something that happened in the store that goes beyond the packaging, it is an experience.

All of these things may push you to take out your cell phone, take a picture or a video, and share it with the rest of the world. Eventually, there will be millions and millions of views. Eventually, there will be many more views than a TV ad and, for sure, much more relevant. The TV ad is me, Pepsi, talking to you, while that piece of content is you user-generating the content and sharing with others, so it's more authentic; it's more meaningful to me looking at you.

Debbie laid out the three key steps of interaction that consumers have with products and brands:

1. The utilitarian need. I buy something because I need it. I buy water because I need to hydrate myself, or I buy a car to go from A to B.

2. Emotional need. Essentially, I buy something because I love it. I buy the pair of shoes because I particularly like them, and it may be brand driven—I like Louboutin. It may be product driven—I like the cashmere, the material, the manufacturing of the specific product. That's emotional. It's you and the product. It's not about others.

3. The semiotic interaction. It's now all of a sudden about what that brand or product is saying about you to the rest of the world. For instance, my jacket or shoes or my watch without hands is saying something to you. It's code. Managing the codes to convey the right messages is key.

In the world of celebrities, creating a specific image is a big part of building a brand. Their wardrobe is part of the code that conveys the image they want to project. Stylist Micaela Erlanger talks about her job as being responsible for the personal image of brands:

> Styling encompasses creating an image, and that can happen a number of different ways. I primarily work with celebrities and am responsible for their personal image for their brand. I'm responsible for what they wear on the red carpet and the message that that sends. It also means consulting with brands and designers, whether it's styling ad campaigns, runway shows for fashion week, or look books. Ultimately, we're image architects. We are creating and sculpting the image of whatever it might be. It's a very creative field. It's a very difficult field because there are so many variables involved, but you can hone in on everything, and if you're a really good stylist, you do it all.
>
> A brand is your public image, and it is the message associated with whatever it is you've created, whether it's the brand for an individual or a brand for a clothing line, and it's about the messaging that's associated with it. That messaging can be very powerful. It can be very transformative if it's quoted the right way. You want your message to be strong and cohesive, and that takes development, and it has to be authentic.
>
> When I'm dealing with celebrities who are on the red carpet, it is the most impactful when it is truly a collaboration. This is where the difference is between fashion brand and a human being. It's a little bit more aspirational, with a fashion brand when you're building an image. With my clients, it is truly an

extension of who they are. It's polished and it's been elevated, but it is a collaboration and it is a natural extension of who they are. It has to be authentic, and without that, it won't be successful. You have to work on a very personal level, and it's a deep collaboration with all parties.

Whether I'm teaching, on panels, or lecturing, a question that inevitably comes up is about how to create a "personal brand." It's simple. Your personal brand is your reputation. However, people try to project who they are through their social media—how they dress, where they are, what they are doing. Social media has made the concept of reputation and personal brand much more complicated.

Author and strategic marketing consultant Dorie Clark talked about a personal brand:

People slag on the term *personal brand* because they think it sounds kind of crass, but it's just a modern coinage. Ultimately, your reputation is the only thing you have. It is the most valuable asset to protect. What do people think about you? How do they describe your character? Your brand is what people say about you when you leave the room.

In my first book, *Reinventing You*, I lay out a three-step process for building your personal brand and handling any reinventions that may come down the line. The first critical step is to understand where you're starting.

How do you do that from a branding perspective? There are a few things that you can do, but at a very foundational level, what are your strengths? What are your weaknesses? What are you good at? This is a little tricky for us to understand. It is very hard for us to have the perspective and judgment to know that what we do is different from other people. I hear from a lot of really talented people, and there'll say, "I can do blah, blah, blah," but so can everyone else. A lot of times people feel like there's nothing special about them.

How do you figure out what is special about you? There's an exercise that I prescribed in *Reinventing You* called the three-word exercise. This is super fast and super easy. What it entails is that over the course of a few days, you reach out to about a half-dozen people that know you reasonably well, and you ask them a very simple question: "If you had to describe me in only three words, what would they be?" It takes a minute for them to do it. Write down their answers. By the time you get to the fourth or the fifth or the sixth person, you are going to start to see some clear patterns in what they are saying.

Odds are it is not going to be so crazy. It's not going to be, oh my God, I've never thought that about myself. If it is, be a little concerned. Most people have a reasonable-enough sense that if they are, let's say, a quiet person, they probably get it. What is extremely useful is what we don't know, and fundamentally cannot know, is what is it about us that other people think is most distinctive about us?

You can do that for almost everybody in your life. You can't do it for yourself because you know too many things about yourself, so you need that external perspective to see what is it that other people are seeing about you and this kind of quick view. When you have that, it begins to give you a sense of what are the strengths and distinctive qualities that you can double down on so that you can then really own it. You can really lean into that aspect of your brand and max it out.

Whether for a product or an individual, branding is creating the images and vocabulary that tell the story, coupled with the distribution strategy to get the message out there.

You can't do "branding" until you are clear what the brand stands for. Many companies confuse branding with doing a lot of advertising and marketing, but until the core message is clear, all the advertising and marketing in the world won't establish a brand identity.

BECOMING A BRAND means that there is something that establishes a differentiated meaning for your product or service that consumers care about—before you begin branding.

For a brand to be successful, the difference must be simple to understand. What does the brand stand for? For example: Apple versus PC (personal computer) is hip versus square. The difference needs to be relevant to the consumer. Their first commercial, "Think Different," set the template and differentiated Apple from all other computers. The Apple commercials, portraying the Mac and PC users, are great examples of illustrating brand differences in an effective way.

A brand needs to be a simple, persuasive idea: "Just do it." The message must be consistent and reinforced wherever and whenever you communicate to your consumers.

People want engagement and emotional attachment, something to connect with. An effective brand story does that. Quest Nutrition is about empowerment. Airbnb is about feeling at home wherever you are. These are universal concepts we can all relate to.

··

Workbook Questions

To begin writing your brand's story, consider the following:

- 💡 Why did you create this product or service? What is the emotional connection to the customer?

- 💡 What is your mission statement?

- 💡 What is the product's unique distinction, talent, or capability? Why should anyone buy this? This is your value proposition and promise to your consumer.

- 💡 What are the emotional attributes and image you want to communicate to your audience? Communicate clearly what you *are*—not what you aren't.

- 💡 Who is your market? How and where do you best communicate with them?

- 💡 What is your strategy for creating brand awareness (PR, marketing, advertising)?

- 💡 How do you constantly reinforce, simplify, and unify your message?

- 💡 Are you consistent in all the ways you reach your consumer and the people within your company?

··

PART FIVE

RUN YOUR IDEAS
LIKE A BUSINESS

13

Are You a Left- or Right-Brain Person? Answer: Neither.

SOME PEOPLE THINK THEY ARE right-brained: creative, perceptive, and intuitive. Others think they are left-brained: logical, methodical, and analytical. The left-brain, right-brain dichotomy came about in 1981 when neuropsychologist Roger W. Sperry won the Nobel Prize for split-brain research. Sperry's work showed that each hemisphere of the brain specializes in certain tasks. For example, the left side of the brain processes analytical and verbal tasks, while the right is responsible for the spatial perception tasks.

Sophisticated brain scans have revealed there is more crosstalk between our brain hemispheres than scientists used to believe. Sperry's theory was proven wrong years ago, but it still holds in popular culture. There are articles, self-help books, and quizzes you can take online to "discover" whether you are a right- or left-brain person.

Whether you think you are more of a businessperson than an artist, the research doesn't change anything; that's who you think you are. However, science tells us that it is not accurate to associate these traits with one side or the other of your brain. There is a lot we don't know regarding what determines an individual's personality, but we do know that left- or right-brain is not a factor.

Logic and creativity go hand in hand because such a large part of being creative is problem solving. Believing you are one way or the other can limit your potential. It can also be an excuse or rationalization for not doing what you don't want to do. "I can't do that. I'm a right-brain person, not a numbers person."

Many people think they have the mental ability to multitask effectively. Who hasn't heard someone claim to be a great multi-tasker? I asked Ben Parr, who did an extensive study regarding attention, what he thought about it.

> There was literally no person who was better at multitask-ing than single-focus tasking. Every single study shows us that we really suck at multitasking. There was another study that found, the ones who consider themselves multitaskers were actually the least effective at switching between tasks, com-pleting tasks, and completing them on time. We really suck at multitasking.

Left brain, right brain: a myth. Multitasking: a myth. It's important to realize how your brain works in order to perform most effectively.

BALANCING ART AND COMMERCE
WHILE PAYING OVERHEAD

You may be an artist, but you also have had to become a boss, negotiator, marketer, and hustler. You can't do it alone.

Zaria Forman said that as her business grew, she had less time for her art:

> I was spending all of my days on email, just responding to peo-ple, and I didn't have time for my art. I needed a studio man-ager; I needed assistants. That was the first really scary step.

Delegating tasks can be really hard when you're used to doing it all on your own. It's not what you have to worry about right off the bat, but it's definitely stuff that happens if you want to be successful. You need to be a boss, and that's hard. It's all a learning process, but it's good to learn new things.

Dennis Crowley struggled to generate income early on:

When we were getting all this press for Foursquare, my dad said, "So what? You can't eat newspapers." I'm like, "You're right. We've got to find some way to generate some revenue off of this," which we've been fortunate to be able to do.

Some days are good. Some days are bad. You win some deals. You lose some deals. Some days you're high-fiving, and some days you're crying in the stairwell.

We had offers to buy us early on, and my dad says, "Dan, I don't know how you can turn these offers down. This is a lot of money for Foursquare." I told him, "We're building this thing that we have to build. We can do something that no one else is going to do." He said, "I can't empathize with you, but I have faith in you. I trust you. You should go out and do this thing."

Discovering what your passion is fuels your commitment to difficult tasks—like staying with or starting a business.

Amy Smilovic had an unlikely career path that led to her starting Tibi. Right after college, she went to work for Ogilvy & Mather advertising. She was there for three years and was then hired by her client American Express. She worked for Amex in New York four years and then got married, to another Amex executive. He got transferred overseas to Hong Kong, which would have meant Amy would have been reporting to him.

That just was not in the cards for me. I love art, I love business, but I really loved clothing and design. I wanted my own business.

I'm so grateful that before doing it, I had my career in advertising and at American Express. I'm glad that I worked at a drugstore when I was in tenth grade. I'm glad I worked in clothing boutiques all through high school. I'm glad I waitressed at the pizza restaurant at the University of Georgia because I feel like I have a broad exposure to things, and I'm so glad that I lived in Hong Kong, in Japan, and saw the rest of the world. I love that I have all those different points to reference because all of that goes into my decision making every day.

How did I know what I was doing? I didn't know what I was doing. I worked off of my own level of common sense and curiosity and asking questions and trying things out. When I got into this business everyone was like, you need to go find a mentor and go ask people about the industry. I talked to this guy who was with Pringle knits in Hong Kong. He said, "Listen, little girl, do not go into this business. You don't want it." Everyone I talked to thinks they're helping you out by telling you what can go wrong. That is not helpful.

Amy wasn't interested in seeking outside money for her business or in growth for the sake of growth and pleasing investors. She wanted to control her company, which directly related to the kind of life she wants to live: she wants to do what she wants to do. Amy explained why she decided to bootstrap her business:

We're constantly reinvesting back into the business because I want the freedom that that allows. I don't think a lot of entrepreneurs lay in bed at night and think, "I would like to grow up one day so I could have like ten guys in Greenwich telling me what to do every day with my designs." That certainly was not what I had in mind.

We get to do what we want. I really do like to live in the here and now. We have a really nice office; people are painting and creating things. I have eight sewers and four pattern makers, and we make things in our office in New York. We don't do it in China because it's cheaper. We actually make it in New York because we can do it and we can feel it.

For me, that is what life is about. I'm doing this business because I love creative things and I love making great things, and I love it when a woman or a man puts on something of ours and feels really great in it. I love how clothing makes me feel. There are just different paths for everyone, but we have chosen to stay private. Yesterday morning I would've said I've regretted it with every bone in my body, but today, I love it. So it's up and down.

Amy made her decision; she favored control and independence over the kind of relationship she would have with a private-equity firm. She had a clear vision of what success looks like for her.

Initially, that may mean you're not making much money yourself because you're reinvesting all the time in your own business, which is how you grow. To many entrepreneurs, it's worth the pain because a lot of people ended up getting venture capital and basically creating a job for themselves, as opposed to creating the company they wanted to build.

Daymond John went from looking for investors to being one on *Shark Tank*. Having been through building FUBU, he knows the high risk of investing, and he wants to be compensated for that:

I always say to anybody that comes on to *Shark Tank* and pitches me that I want to take 30 percent of the company. There are some deals I want to take 70 percent. The ones I want to take 70 percent or 80 percent of the company are people who don't have any proof of concept. They come in there with this great idea and all this theory. They haven't sold out one thing.

Why do I have to take that amount? Because I have to take a gamble. We're going to have to learn this market on my dollars. I have my own ideas that I can own 100 percent of. Yours just happens to be something I think there's a value. Anybody who wants deals, you have to have sales and proof of concept. It doesn't have to be a lot. It just has to be some form of a conversion where not your grandma or not your friends are buying your product. Absolute total strangers.

The earlier in your business you seek money, the more you will have to give up to get it. All venture capital is risky. Early-stage venture capital looks for big returns because they are taking the biggest risk by investing at the early stages of the company. The more you've established a proof of concept, the better the deal you can negotiate for yourself. The important thing to realize is, as you take in outside investment, it most likely won't be just once. The more capital you take on, the more control you will ultimately relinquish. That's not necessarily bad; it depends on how you view it. If you have big ambition, the cost may be big and outside capital essential to the idea happening. It's important to be fully aware of the terms, coupled with the knowledge that private equity is in it to make a profit. Their idea of profitable and worthwhile may be different from yours. There are going to be bumps in the road. There are going to be things that don't work. Things are going to cost more and take longer than you anticipated. It can get rough out there.

There are different ways of running and financing a business, but don't abdicate responsibility because you think you are creative and not a businessperson. Being aware is essential so you won't be taken advantage of. Be smart about how you spend what you have. Be creative about how you face the challenges of starting and growing a business.

It is important to find people who complement your unique skills, which may be a person who knows how to run a business or is a talented manager. Learn about yourself so you know where you can yield the most value to what you are doing, and try to find support in those other areas that are essential but not necessarily done well by you.

When you enter the business of the business, creativity plays a significant part. Deals are created. Whether you are trying to bootstrap, attract individual investors, gain venture capital, or be acquired, the story you can tell about your company becomes a tremendous asset. There are reasons and reactions to whichever financial path you choose. However, if you are passionate about your business and are creating something that is an extension of who you are and your core beliefs, you will want to maintain control. There are strategies and disciplines that can help you achieve that. You need to know how to determine your value.

Workbook Questions

- How will you obtain financing for your business?

- What are you willing to give up to get the money you want?

- Is your business born of a true passion or mission, or are you primarily interested in making money?

- If you answered "passion" or "mission," how would you define it?

- How important is maintaining control of your business and why?

14

Determining Your Value

A BOTTLE OF WATER SELLS for ninety-nine cents in a store. Is that what it is worth? Value is determined by context and the "given circumstances." It is one thing if you are walking down the street in New York and stop in a store to buy a bottle, one to three and half dollars depending on the kind of bottled water. If another store charged ten dollars for the same bottle, you would think that is outrageous—it's not worth ten dollars. Let's change the given circumstances. You are in the desert. Would you pay ten, twenty, fifty dollars? You need that bottle of water to stay alive. What about five hundred? Five thousand? The given circumstances, the context in which you are making the decision, can dramatically change the perception of value.

I once thought things had an intrinsic value. I looked at the stock-market pages, all those columns of numbers, price/earnings ratios, shares sold: It certainly seemed like everything was so carefully calculated to arrive at a certain value. If a person could somehow crack those codes, what the numbers were telling us, we could arrive at a way to invest in the market without risk or at least very little risk. Numbers don't lie—I thought.

It wasn't until many years later that I realized numbers are words that form a language. Those words can be used to create fact or fiction. There are many people who are quite creative with the stories they tell with numbers, and like all great story-tellers it's ultimately the emotional engagement that takes in the audience. Like fiction, it's the illusion that is created that people believe in or don't believe in that ultimately determines the value. There is no intrinsic value in words. It's how they are put together and how they are interpreted and whether they are believed. It's the same with most things, including art, fashion, and bottled water. Establishing value can be challenging, yet very important to success.

Vanessa Friedman elaborates:

There is just way too much stuff. It has affected how we value expensive clothing as well as inexpensive clothing. I think it has actually turned people off to such an extent they just don't want any more stuff at all. My kids, they have jeans or leggings, T-shirts, and sweatshirts. Whenever we ask, "What do you want for your birthday?" they want a trip or they want to go to Governor's Ball or they want some new piece of technology or a subscription to a streaming service. I can count on one hand the number of times they've asked for a piece of clothing or an object. They're really not that brand interested.

When there's that much stuff, everything ceases to have the same meaning. When I was growing up, my mother saved and saved to get a Gucci bag. I remember being ten or twelve when she brought it home and we all looked at it. Then it sat in its soft bag pouch, and she probably still has it. It was a real thing that meant something to her and meant something about where she had gotten to in her career because she was working, which was pretty rare at that time. She bought it, and it was an investment she made over time. We seem to have really lost that understanding, and I think that is bad in multiple ways.

There is an abundance of product, not just in fashion, but almost every category. It is hard for something to be considered special when there is so much of everything that is so accessible, often twenty-four hours a day, seven days a week. A product has to be distinctive in some way to create the perception of value. Otherwise, it's a commodity.

If you want to make a living with your ideas, you need to figure out what to charge for your work or creations. It is up to you to determine how much you charge and up to the marketplace to validate it—or not.

ESTABLISHING YOUR RATE

In the early days of the music, movie, and fashion industries, talent was not valued and creative people were taken advantage of. There was a large schism between the creative and the "suits" who controlled the money. That has changed as the businesses became big businesses and the creative talent did, too.

I wrote a play about one of the pioneers of rock and roll, a black man named Lloyd Price. Lloyd wrote and performed a song called "Lawdy Miss Clawdy" that sold over 1 million copies, an unheard-of number at that time, a first for a record by a teenager. That song changed the course of the music business and is considered one of the cornerstone songs of rock and roll.

Young artists would record a song, and they would get roughly 2.5 percent of the sales after all the expenses, which were taken out of their side. It was more money than they had ever had, so they thought they were doing well. They didn't have the business sense to realize they were being taken advantage of. It still happens. Creative fields are prime targets because, at least initially, it's about the passion and pursuit of the art. In the context of what they were making before, it seemed like they were doing well. In Lloyd's case, he went from making $27.36 a week digging trenches for septic tanks to performing for $8,000 a week in a few months. Seems like a lot until you realize how much more the label was making. Lloyd was unusual. He did another first: he was an entrepreneur, the first musical artist to start his own label, because "that music math didn't make any sense to me."

How do you value your work? How do you establish your price? Artist, author, and illustrator Oliver Jeffers, who has written such children's favorites as *How to Catch a Star* and *The Incredible Book Eating Boy*, talks about the difficulty of advocating for yourself as an artist and asking for the money you deserve to build your career:

> That's a very difficult thing to do. If you put on an exhibition, you can put whatever price you want on a painting, and people say, "That's the amount of money it's worth." But is it actually worth that until somebody else is willing to part with their money? So it's this balancing act between what you feel in reality, what you feel ideally you want, and where somebody else will fit into that paradigm, who's willing to actually give that money. It's this constant adjustment of those different forces. For commercial illustration, it's educating people in the value of what it is to get somebody who's going to create both art and concepts. There has been this mentality for a long time that that's not as important as the people who deal with the finances of something.
>
> It's a slow build, and you are only as good as your last project. When I first graduated, I spent a lot of time making portfolios and putting attention into a website that I was showing people and generating this idea of the value and the worth of my work.
>
> After a certain number of years, that goes away because you don't have the time to do that, because you're making other projects, and then those projects become your résumé; they become your portfolio. That just builds and builds. But a big part of it for me was about ten years ago. I realized that I was not happy being a gun for hire in the commercial world because I had all these other projects I wanted to do and say

and make myself, and I'm being hired to solve somebody else's visual problems, at that point the most financially lucrative aspect of my career. It comes down to how much you value what you have to say and how you rank that with financial security.

Oliver was doing very well as an illustrator. He had a number of good commercial clients and had gotten to the point of being paid quite well. Then he came to the conclusion that he wanted his own expression out there. He wanted to solve his own visual problems, instead of dealing with a client, and establish his value as an artist on his own terms.

How does an artist know what to charge? It's not a parts-and-labor business, although that's a part of it, as in the cost of materials, but the X factor is what can you, as a creative, charge for your talent.

There is that first time an artist sells their work, but there is no guidebook to help you establish your value. Value is confirmed if someone buys it. Zaria Forman had no idea what to charge when she was first presenting her work for sale, a painting that was six by eight feet. She talked about it with her mother and spoke to a couple of galleries in her town. She wanted to find a general range to start. What you charge, and this is true in any career, is based on where you are in your career. You don't want to start off with too high a price because you don't have anything to back that up. She asked for $5,000. I asked Zaria how she felt about asking that price for her painting:

I was terrified. I did not think that I was worth it. It's really scary. But I think the more you value yourself and your work, then the more other people recognize your value. So I think it is important to oftentimes shoot higher than you think you should go for, and that allows for negotiation. Think about what price you would not give up that piece of art or whatever you're creating. That's your baseline. Then ask for something above that. In the art world, there's always some negotiation.

It was really exciting for me, to make $5,000 right after graduating college. And then it just grows from there, so once you set a price and you make a sale, you're done. That's your price point. And then the more shows you get, the more recognition you get, you start building up your résumé with write-ups and exhibitions, and then you can start increasing the price incrementally.

I asked her how much that same painting would cost now. She smiled broadly: the answer was $100,000.

My gallery always prefers to raise the prices about 10 percent every solo show, maybe every year and a half, which is not enough for me. I'm always arguing to go more, more, more. Part of the reason I can argue is because they're selling really well. If they're selling like that, clearly, we can charge more. It's always a give-and-take and a conversation with my gallery now. It used to just be me on my own and talking to my mom and getting as much advice as I can from the people around me, which is so important, in growing a career. Find those people who can be your mentors, and keep them around, and that's where you learn so, so much.

How to establish your value and reflect that in your pricing is an obstacle that most people who start their own business will have to overcome. When you first get a paying job, on the one hand, you don't want to price yourself out and you want the gig. On the other hand, you don't want to undersell yourself. I asked makeup artist Daniel Martin how he navigated that before he had an agent:

Before, I would just accept whatever rate the producer gave me. If you shot an ad job for Macy's, this was the general rate.

If you did an ad campaign for Balmain or whatever, that's the rate. There's not a lot of money in fashion anymore. There's a lot of "Could you do this for the images, and we'll throw you a bag?"

It depends on the job and depends on the client and depends on how much you really want that job. Because there's a lot of freebies in the business, and if you have a relationship with someone, you want to be able to support them and then hope that they can pay it forward to you next time.

Because of Instagram, there's a lot of people that do gigs for the gram; that's what we call it. Would you want to do the gig for the gram? That is you work with someone who can't afford to pay you, but you can use her image on your social to try to drum up whatever business it is. That's something that I don't deal with because I don't care about my Instagram.

There was times when I would have to hunt down clients, and holy shit, my rent is due, what am I going to do? We've all been there. I feel like that's part of the journey.

Designers are often asked for clothing for free. They or their publicists (or both) think there is great value for designers to have their work seen on them at major events. Some designers, categorically, won't do it: "This is what I do for a living."

Mick Jagger wanted a suit from a friend of mine, but he didn't want to pay, and he certainly had the money. My friend wouldn't do it because he didn't think the exchange value was worth it. When you're dealing with celebrities, on the one hand they are a great billboard for your work and you might get great publicity. On the other hand, my friend didn't want to establish that he gives his clothing or services away. "I value my work more than that, plus, how am I going to pay my rent?"

Dan Sullivan
on the Psychology of Pricing

When Dan Sullivan started his business, Strategic Coach, he wasn't selling a physical product, nor was he selling a service that had an established business model out there. He made it clear that one of the most important skills of being an entrepreneur is around the psychology of pricing. You want the work and the customer, but you also want a certain price. It's a big challenge to establish the pricing for what you do.

The more you're in the entrepreneurial realm, the more that you realize that pricing is almost purely psychological. I have this concept, "the double sale." The price, first of all, has to be sold to you. As the entrepreneur, I'm thinking about a project, and I'm going to put a price on the project. The first thing I have to do is sell myself on the price. This is really crucial because a lot of entrepreneurs actually are putting out a price that they're not sold on. When they get a negative reaction, they immediately fold and then undercut themselves. One of the biggest skills as an entrepreneur is to sell yourself at a price that you're going to hold to and you would be willing to walk if you don't get that price.

The number-one growth vehicle for entrepreneurs is to actually continually create higher and higher levels of pricing. Then of course, you develop the abilities to actually deliver at that price. You're not selling air here. You're actually selling skill, but I think what draws the skill out and what draws the capability is your commitment to a particular pricing level.

You grow with that, and then you reach one level, and then you have to go to a higher pricing level. Just to give you an example, I just added this up that in 1982 to get paid $1,000 was a really good pay day, $1,000. You have to take inflation into account where the $1,000, let's say it was $2,500 today. This year, I get paid slightly over $200,000 a day.

I'm working almost these same number of days, and so when you look, there's a one-hundred times increase in what I'm getting paid for. In some ways, I'm a lot more comfortable, my present level of getting paid than I was getting paid back then when I was one hundredth of the price. All along, if you measure, well how did that happen? It's just one level to another level.

Every time you get to a level, you sell yourself first, that you're going to charge more, and then you put the price out there. There's a skill that develops around. Oftentimes when they teach business courses, they don't talk about the psychology of pricing. It's one of the things most miss, from all business training, because they think that there's a price that's set by the marketplace.

Yet everybody who is great doesn't pay any attention to the pricing of the marketplace. They only pay attention to their own pricing. I think that pricing is probably the magic thread of successful entrepreneurs, that there is a freedom with pricing and it all depends upon your ability. Every time you raise your price, you're taking a risk, and then you respond to the risk by increasing the value, increasing your skill level.

My formula for pricing is that the price scares you plus 20 percent. I always get a big laugh in my workshops when I say this. First of all, "Between the two of you, you or the prospect, who's the one who's scared of the price? You are. He does not know about the price yet so he can't be scared." So this scary price thing is strictly the one that's going on in your head. Then I said, "Let's say you put that price out there," and the person says, "Well, that's really reasonable," then you kick yourself because the price wasn't high enough, and that's why I add the extra 20 percent on top. It's Sullivan's rule of pricing.

I've had people have a nervous breakdown and I said, "Just try it." Even if the person says no, you've just acquired a marketing ability. Let's say the price you put out there, if you want me, it's going to cost you $250,000 for the day, and the person says no.

Well, it's just a no, and I don't have to do it to another person. Maybe I'll adjust my price for the next person, but every person that that first person talks to says, "Well, you know, he's really expensive. He charges $250,000 a day." That person might talk to thirty other individuals, and one of those people might call me up and say, "I understand you are $250,000 a day," and I say, "Yeah." I say, "There may be some adjustments depending upon special requirements."

Even when you get a no at a high price, it's very good marketing because you're establishing a reputation at a price that would really be enormously attractive and rewarding to you.

It's a very big challenge for entrepreneurs to establish their pricing. They have no idea what they should or could charge. When you are starting out, the price weighs heavier because you want the business, you need the business, yet you want a certain price.

Understanding the psychology of pricing and knowing what that means, not just to the customer but to yourself, is key. Joe Polish told me about his theory on different ways to get paid:

There are five ways you get paid, in no particular order:

1. Money, that's one way to get paid. If that's the only way that you get paid, then the business you're in is prostitution.
2. The second way to get paid is people appreciate you. Appreciation.
3. Another way to get paid is people refer you.
4. People utilize whatever your skills are.
5. The fifth way that you get paid is it enhances you.

When I first got into business, I would read all these books of how much is my time worth per hour, and I would always find myself focusing on activities and people that didn't pay the most money, but it was interesting to me. So when I would read all these books about making money, the books would focus on reward. I'd be like, "Well, you know, like that's not the main thing to me." So what is the number-one criteria for me? How I involve myself with people.

Money is important to me, but it is at the end of the list. One of the things that I learned early on was that you can have an E.L.F. business, which is easy, lucrative, and fun, or you can have a H.A.L.F. business, which is hard, annoying, lame, and frustrating. I want E.L.F. relationships. I want people that are easy, lucrative, and fun because you can have a hard, annoying, lucrative, and frustrating life. Not all money is created equal.

Certain money is like blood money: you're literally trading your life for things that aren't enjoyable when you actually can be doing things that are quite enjoyable.

So I tend to create standards about who I hang out with, what I spend my time on, what I end up learning. The sooner you learn in life that whatever you're putting up with or whatever you have in your life is your own creation. You are 100 percent responsible for where you are at in your life, and you're not entitled to anything. I learned that money earned ethically is a by-product of value creation. So until I can create value for somebody, I don't deserve anything.

There is financial value and there are values, what you stand for as a person. Money can be a seductive force and change one's values. However, one's core values often resonate through everything they do. They are who they are regardless of the situation. Kathy Ireland talked to me about protecting her values:

You need to know your boundaries. You need to figure out what are your values, what's important to you, what are you willing to be fired for, what will you walk away from? At some point or another, you are going to be placed in those positions where you need to make those decisions. If you've thought about it ahead of time, it's a lot easier to know what you're going to do when you're thrust in that situation. I encourage you to put some boundaries in place to protect your values because they will be challenged.

When I started modeling, it was a time where there were a lot of young girls, and my heart broke for a lot of these girls and their families. I think they just didn't understand the pressures they were putting on themselves, and they thought, "Oh, you come to New York City—you instantly become a star."

And there was pressure. If they didn't do some prestigious work, they didn't want to go home. There'd be photographers that would cause them to believe you have to do this and do that and that you've got to compromise here and there to get ahead. It's simply not true. But people will prey on others, to satisfy themselves. It's important to be alert to that and to know what you're willing to walk away from.

Breaking down your costs—the time, labor, materials, and overhead—is all the same whether you are a clothing designer, life coach, architect, author, or accountant. It is just like every other kind of work. Being an artist requires a certain skill and talent set, but the protocols about making a living at it are the same no matter what it is you decide to do. And it's important to understand that because so many people put up these different barriers between the disciplines, and they don't really exist. However, if you don't value yourself, you're in a great position to be taken advantage of by others. The difference is how you value what you do, who you are, and what you are willing to walk away from.

WIN-WIN NEGOTIATING

People are reluctant to ask for a raise or for even more responsibility. Negotiation is a skill, and the more you practice it, the better you get at it. But you need to value yourself and not be afraid to ask for what you think you are worth. However, you will also need to demonstrate your value rather than simply declare it.

Fran Hauser
on How to Ask for More

An important way to prepare for negotiating is to put yourself in the shoes of the other person. What are you hoping to get, and how can you justify what you are asking for? What do they hope to get from the negotiation? What are your must-haves? What are you willing to give up?

The first is you need to understand what your market rate is. You do that by talking to peers at other organizations. That's where meet-ups, events, and trade associations are really important, so that you can develop relationships with these people and talk openly about your compensation. You'll be helping each other.

Make recruiters your best friend. I remember when I was at Time, Inc., I would take recruiters out for coffee a couple times a year because they are filling roles like the one that you're in so they know what your market rate is. If you go into the conversation with your manager armed with this data, not only does it make you more confident, but you're also more likely to get the raise because your manager is going to be like, wow, they actually did the research. Understanding your market rate is a big part of it. Be clear about the value that you add to the organization. When you're asking for a raise, obviously it's such a personal thing, but what does the company stand to gain by retaining you?

Think about it from the company's perspective and be creative about bringing up ideas that you have that might be new, like business ideas or revenue opportunities. A good time to ask for a raise is if you've just had a really big win at the company. Don't wait until your performance review because I've given so many performance reviews over the years, and as a manager you're given 3 percent of the total of all of the salaries and your department, so you have 3 percent to play with.

Women tend to negotiate more effectively if they're negotiating on behalf of someone else. So if you're negotiating on behalf of your best friend, you could clearly see the value they add to the company and you love them so much that you're going to go to bat for them, channel that toward yourself. Love yourself enough that you're going to go to bat for yourself. Have a lot of confidence. Own it.

If you don't ask, the answer is always no. It goes back to, what's the worst-case scenario? You get a no. If you get to no, is there a networking organization that you want to join? If it's a $1,000 annual subscription, ask for that because they just said no to your salary increase. There are other things that you can ask for that you can keep in your hip pocket.

The other thing is about stepping up to opportunities. Men tend to apply for positions if they're 60 percent qualified, whereas women feel they need to be 100 percent qualified. The first thing we do as women is say, "I don't have that experience." You talk yourself out of applying. Don't do that. If you are 60 percent qualified, go for it. What's the worst case? You get to polish up your résumé, practice interviewing, and you meet the hiring manager. It's a networking opportunity. Even if you don't get the job, you're showing that you are ambitious and driven; you're getting on senior management's radar. There are so many good things that can come out of it. I encourage especially the women to close this wage gap. Women make 80 percent of what men make; women of color make 63 percent of what men make. Companies have to do their part, but we also have to do our part by asking for more.

If you talk to any negotiating expert, they will tell you that the most important thing when you're negotiating if you want to get to a successful outcome is showing empathy and try to get into the other person's head and understand what's important to them. What are they trying to get out of this negotiation? The way you do that is by starting the conversation with questions and listening, as opposed to what a lot of us tend to do—go into a conversation so focused on what I need to get out of it—versus if you just take a breath and start with "What's important to you in this?" It ends up turning into a win-win outcome. Even if you end up spending most of the time talking about the other person because then they end up trusting you. It creates a psychologically safe environment where you can have a productive conversation.

Empathy is understanding or feeling what another person feels from their point of view. It can form a powerful bond between friends and be a powerful tool for business. If you are negotiating for a raise, or trying to raise money for your business, empathy comes in when you take the focus off of what you hope to get and try to understand the other person's needs, what's important to them, and what they want to get out of the situation. By definition, negotiations are between at least two people. They are an attempt to reach an equitable compromise based on the positions of those involved. What do you value, and where do you establish your boundaries so you don't violate them; that is, what are the "nonnegotiables"? Sabin Howard places a high value on his skill and his art. His awareness of who he is and where he fits in is essential to arriving at the price he wants.

> I strongly believe in values. I strongly believe that the world is hierarchical and not everyone is at the same level. When you go to a meeting, where you fit into that is very relevant to how much money and how many jobs you're going to get when you walk out the door.
>
> If you're higher on the scale and are a hard ass like me, when you go to a meeting, and I'm very polite, I'm very gracious about it, but nobody will walk on me. I will walk away with a lot more because I believe in myself and I believe in what I am doing. You have to legitimize in yourself, your perception of reality. Perception drives reality.
>
> When I made my first sculptures and my first drawings, I worked on my skill. Basically ten to twelve hours a day, six days a week. I have an obsession. This is what I'm going to do, and I will stick to it. Then your craft goes up, the self-criticism goes up with it, and you keep driving your product up. You have to get really good at your product or your skill. Then when you go to the market, you're in a very good place because you believe in yourself and you can say, "Okay, I'm worth this much." Skill first. Then you believe in yourself.

It all comes down to value and values. That ties directly into self-worth. You can't establish a positive self-worth if you don't value who you are and what you offer. To succeed in business, it is also important to have a real understanding of the value and importance of another person's experience and acknowledging their value, which takes us back to empathy. Establishing your rate is the combination of self-worth, plus empathy, combined with the knowledge of the marketplace you are in.

* * *

Workbook Questions

💡 What do you value and why?

💡 What boundaries are you not willing to compromise?

💡 How would you determine what to charge for what you do?

💡 Is there anything distinctive about what you do that you could charge more for?

💡 What are the key takeaways regarding negotiating?

💡 Do you consider yourself an empathic person? If so, how is that expressed?

* * *

15

How to Keep It Going

WHEN I WAS IN COLLEGE, a group of us were talking about what we wanted to do when we graduated. One of the guys said he wanted to be a writer, but "I'm not going to sell out and write a best seller."

I was struck by the naïveté of his announcement and challenged him, "There is another reason you're not going to write a best seller."

His jaw stiffened, "What do you mean?"

"You haven't written anything yet, and you're already declaring you would not 'sell out and write a best seller'? Do you think it's easy? Even if you don't like their book, anybody that writes a best seller has worked hard just to get it written, and then they have to sell it. It's a lot of hard work."

Most of you reading this have seen a movie, read a book, or seen a design or painting in a gallery and thought, *I could've done that*. What's the distinguishing difference? They actually did it. It's a lot easier to criticize than do the work and put yourself out there. So what is the best way to approach your career so you up the odds of having the success you want? The first step is to commit. Actually do it. And keep doing it. And keep it going even when you hit obstacles, get criticized, and feel alone. A big part of any creative career is perseverance.

Oliver Jeffers discussed how he kicked himself into high gear early in his career:

I always tried to see how little I could get away with doing. I was like that right up until the very end of my art college, when I realized that, yeah, I can get away with as little as I want and pull the wool over people's eyes—but is that actually what I want? The penny dropped for me whenever I realized that nobody else was going to do any of these things for me. I probably could skip by doing very little, but I would've ended up disappointed with myself for that. Something clicked into gear right around the beginning of my final year in college. I decided if I'm going to do this, I'm going to do it as best as I possibly can.

Something else happened right when I was in an art college. My mother passed away. I was in the right frame of mind to receive the lesson that was being shown to me: Life is very, very fragile, and we are all going to die at some point. It was that simple. If I do want to do all these things, I better get cracking. It was the combination of those two things that just something came together, and I was just this absolute rocket of productivity, not taking no for an answer and just doing it. I adopted the mantra "I'll sleep when I'm dead."

Oliver uses his artistic talents to create fine art, books, posters, limited-edition prints, and collectibles. In other words, he has multiple income streams that he has created to keep his career going. Oliver not only creates art but also created a business model to market and sell what he does so he can keep doing it.

Dorie Clark is an author, public speaker, and consultant. At her core, she is an entrepreneur who makes a living with her ideas. Dorie's strategy keeps her career going by monetizing her ideas on a number of different fronts, as she told me:

I encourage people to think about building multiple income streams so that you are mitigating risk and maximizing the chance to have opportunity. How do you do this? Even if you have a day job as one income stream, it is useful to be pursuing side projects because they can sometimes go in interesting directions. They can help you meet new people. And they can be an extra revenue stream. In my business, I have developed nine income streams that are operating simultaneously, and they're not distractions.

They all are helping to feed each other. I do consulting work, coaching work, write books. I have paid keynote speeches, do business school teaching, and get affiliate income from promoting products for partners. I do live workshops, masterminds, and online courses. All of these things feed into each other. If somebody enters at one of these places, they in fact may not just stop there. It becomes a flywheel of business if you can create this for yourself through different product lines. There are lots of ways to wrap it in, and all of those things can ultimately help each other and help you get more financial freedom.

KILL THE COMPETITION

One of the big fears creatives have is getting copied. This is true in design, tech, and any business where creating something new provides a competitive advantage. However, that competitive advantage goes away quickly if the company doesn't continue to iterate and innovate. Vindigo was one of the first and most innovative tech companies developing content for mobile phones in 1999. They were visionary in terms of what mobile phones would eventually become, laden with apps. They grew rapidly and were bought by a Japanese company in 2004. Vindigo went out of business by 2008. Like most tech companies, they were in a fiercely competitive market. Dennis Crowley elaborates:

In the product world, if we made something successful, everyone in the world just copied it. The only way that you succeed is you make something and then you make it better. Then you make it better after that, and you make it better after that. The thing just has to keep constantly getting better. I don't know of any company that just made one thing and sat back and they're like, "Look at this. We made this thing two years ago, and we're the greatest." You've just got to keep iterating on top of it. Otherwise, someone will just come along and take it from you.

Vindigo is a classic example of a company that was super early. They invented the future. They paved the way for all the stuff that I'm doing. I'm super motivated by and inspired by them, and there are probably a hundred—a thousand—other start-ups that were also inspired by them. They sold to a Japanese company in 2004 and were out of business four years later.

This is true of everything. Like Friendster. Friendster comes along, owns a space, and can't figure out how to dominate it, so MySpace comes along. MySpace comes along, dominates that for a while, before Facebook comes along. Now we're in this point where everyone says, "Well, who can disrupt Facebook?"

There have been a whole bunch of things that have come along that had a good chance of disrupting Facebook. It just happened that Facebook bought them all. Instagram, WhatsApp. People asked, "Why are they paying $19 billion for that?" Because that's the thing that can be a real headache for them if it's left unchecked for a long time. That's why you see these big acquisitions.

It happens in all businesses. TD Ameritrade was acquired by Charles Schwab. Tiffany was acquired by LVMH to counter their main competitor, Richemont, which acquired Cartier. Mobile networks buy other mobile networks, and the same with cable and media companies.

Josh Sapan says that what's occurring now in the TV industry from a business point of view is there's increased competition between cable television, Netflix, and Amazon Prime. Amazon Prime bought the back catalog of HBO, so on the Internet, one can find *The Wire* and *The Sopranos* and everything that's two years old. From the creative point of view, there's going to be, increasingly, TV material that is more nuanced, that people pay closer attention to, and that is building on story.

Amazon, Netflix, and Hulu are just a few of the services that have entered into the fierce competition for our attention. Apple TV is entering the market. Disney bought Marvel and will put a dent in Netflix because Disney will distribute the blockbuster Marvel films and pull them from the other outlets. Dorie Clark has a strategy.

> What you actually need to do is outlast other people. This is the competitive differentiator. Podcasts are not going away. Video blogging, that's not going away. If you decide that you want to participate in that, is it harder, in terms of the sheer numbers of competitors, as compared to five years ago or ten years ago? But the fact is most people quit. That is the key part.
>
> There was a ten-year longitudinal study of podcasts. It showed that the average podcast lasted six months and twelve episodes before its creator quit. That's it. So many people are starting podcasts, but not that many people are staying with podcasts. If you outlast people, if you are willing to be more persistent, if you are willing to keep going when other people are giving up, that means that you are dramatically winnowing the competition and you don't need to worry so much about, oh, what's the hot new channel?

Many people start things. Few people stay with them. Perseverance and tenacity are key elements to keep your business going. It's a daily ritual, knowing what you have to do to survive.

Survival can be a big motivator. Hillary Sterling talked about the difficulty of surviving in the NYC restaurant business:

> I'm on display all day long every day. As in the same, I'm creating a dish and not everyone's going to like it, and sometimes you have to take risks. Some days I'm better at risk taking, and some days I'm terrible at it. I know I could put on the dish that was on last year and it would be successful, but I'm refusing to do so because I'm challenging myself.
>
> There are twenty thousand restaurants in New York City. I have to prove myself to get you to come back every time. If I have a bad day and I lose a guest, I lost money, and the most important thing about a restaurant is that it's consistent and you know what you're going to get every time. Same thing with a designer: we all stick with the same things because I know I can walk in there and purchase something and it's going to fit me in the same way it did last time. I need those carrots to taste the same.
>
> But I'm on display and sometimes, I don't want to prove myself. I do not want to fight today, and then you remind yourself that every day you have to fight. It's New York City. I need two hundred guests every day, and on the weekends we do six hundred people and if I don't have those six hundred people, we won't survive. It totally sucks, but you get used to it.

I asked Dan Sullivan how he would describe the profile of a successful entrepreneur. He answered:

> When you are talking about the profile of the entrepreneur, there are two outstanding qualities. One is the stamina that they have. You are talking about decades, so there has to be enormous stamina. The other quality is perseverance. In my case, I have very good communication qualities, I have very good delegation qualities, but I have to tell you the number-one

thing that I am most confident in is that I am completely and totally relentless. I will never stop.

I will stop at a certain point, when my number comes up, but when I die, I'm going to be in the middle of my biggest project. I am relentless. I will not stop. I will not stop learning. I will not stop improving. I will not stop experimenting. I am totally convinced of that.

Roy Wood Jr. talked about competition:

In comedy, it's hard enough to get this far. If you take a minute and look over your shoulder, there are probably forty people waiting to replace me. I have to be funny. I have to be funnier. I have to be more creative. Because there are fewer spots to perform. Comedy clubs are closing. There are fewer opportunities to get on TV. You can do five minutes on late night, or you can get on and do an hour special.

Not only that, but the comedic palette of customers is changing. If you ask someone to name you their top ten comedians, I guarantee five of them will be YouTubers, or somebody that does sketches on Instagram. For me as a performer, it's annoying that if I don't get this right, somebody else can take my spot. You can't have my spot. I worked too hard. I'm going to go out here and do my damnedest to be sure you don't.

I operate from the place of not wanting to fail; it's not so much wanting to succeed. People say, "Keep going until you see the light at the end of the tunnel." For me, the light at the end of the tunnel is the train coming to run me over. In my brain, that's the train. So I have to go into the darkness, even if I don't completely feel like I know where I'm landing; you jump and figure it out on the way down.

There's more to be lost in being afraid than there is to be bolder with your choices. That doesn't mean the fear isn't there. I'm horrified. But I know if I don't nail this, then everything I've built is gone.

EXPECT THE UNEXPECTED

It is much easier to start a business than it is to build it and even harder to sustain it. I asked Kathy Ireland, who has built a multi-billion-dollar global business how she saw the process of building her brand:

> Brand building is hard work, and if anybody tells you otherwise, I need to learn from them. We've had some difficult times. When we first started selling socks, we were in a handful of sporting goods stores before a major retailer started carrying our brand. When we first started, we were happy to sleep in airports to save money. Whatever material thing you've got to give up to live your dream, it's not a sacrifice; it's a bold investment. And that bold investment made it for us. We sold 100 million pair of socks.
>
> We started selling to a major retailer. The CEO calls one day to inform me that the socks were a blowout; the product is moving out faster than it's coming in, so they asked for exclusivity. We had some questions and hesitations, we did research, we liked them, and we grew our brand there to include a complete line of apparel and accessories. As the brand grew, the spending grew, and we had bigger, fancier offices than we truly needed. The airport sleepovers were long gone. Our banks and financial advisers assured us that we were spending far below the norm for a company of our size. Besides, we had a contract that would guarantee security for many years to come.
>
> Then one day we get a call, and it seems that this retailer was having some challenges. And the next thing, this $40 billion giant upon whom our team was dependent was filing for bankruptcy. Then I get a call from the bank, asking to have lunch, and they were politely referring to this as "the situation." I had enjoyed lunch with a bank on many occasions, always engaging, getting to know them, sharing our business plan. This time it was so different. It was ice cold. While reaching for the credit card, one of

the kind fatherly bankers smiles and says, "You know, we can take away all your homes if this doesn't work out."

I should have known better. At that time, we had seventy members with families on our payroll; we were in debt. It was like *Groundhog Day*, starting all over from the ground up again. Those days were pretty grim. My heart still breaks for all the people who lost their jobs, but it caused us to learn some powerful lessons and to not let it defeat or destroy us. You learn from it, and you get back up again.

When you are hit with that kind of financial wallop, how do keep you going? I asked Kathy if there were a times when she was wondering if it was all worth it. Her take:

We had bills to pay. That was very motivating. We believed in what we were doing. What I learned from some of those earlier businesses that I tried and failed is if I didn't have a passion for it, I wasn't going to stick around when things got difficult. That's why it's important that you believe and love what you're doing, because then it doesn't feel like you're coming to work. It can be hard, but you know what you're doing is a good thing and you're putting something good out there.

Kathy Ireland is essentially saying, "Work hard, work smart, be careful, and keep evolving."

KEEP EVOLVING

A recurring theme I hear is "the company you started often evolves into something quite different." I asked Randi Zuckerberg if that evolution is a desirable quality in business.

Totally. Very few people, when you look at their company years later, are anything like what they originally put on paper. That's part of what makes the entrepreneurial journey so exciting.

You know that the place you end up is going to be nothing like how you started, but you're going to learn a lot in the process. You're going to learn a lot about how you run a business, how people view your product, and what they connect with you about.

As you get older, you realize that everything in life is maintenance. That's also true about your business. It's maintenance. When I started in film and video production, every category was expensive; buying a camera or setting up an editing room was a major financial decision. That has changed dramatically. People shoot with their phones; they can edit on their laptop. The technology has gone through seismic changes. One can lament or embrace the changes, but if you don't evolve, you won't survive.

Dylan Lauren renovated her store to keep it moving forward:

We are literally on our third renovation in thirteen years. We get so many customers. I don't ever want to see this store not become a shining candy jar, so we have to keep it current. Otherwise, you're letting go of your showpiece for people. It's maintenance.

Simon Sinek did an internal renovation. He began his professional life in advertising. He was entrepreneurial and even started his own company. But then he made a life-altering change to what he is doing now. I asked Simon what compelled him to make that pivot.

I ran out of love for the thing that I was doing. I lost passion, and I didn't understand it because I was doing the same thing that I used to do, but I didn't love it anymore. And because life was superficially good, I was embarrassed by this. So I kept it to myself, and things got darker and darker and darker because I couldn't figure it out.

I made this discovery that is based on the biology of human decision making. There are three components that are essential to all of passion in our lives and companies. If I ask you what you do, you can tell me. If I asked you how you do it, most of you can show your résumé and the things that are your strengths. But if I ask you why you do what you do, that's a much more difficult question. The problem is, you need all three. Most people don't know why they do what they do, including me. So I realized we have to know all three pieces, and that was the missing piece. I became obsessed with that piece. I learned my "why" to inspire people to do the things that inspire them.

I became obsessed with spreading this idea. My passion was rejuvenated. What made me go all in is that when I started to see the impact it had on my life, and when I shared it with my friends, I saw the impact that it had on their lives.

The excitement of spreading this message was way more appealing than going back and doing what I used to be doing. When you actually have a cause that you believe in, these kinds of decisions seem risky to everybody else, but to you they become obvious.

Do you have to become an entrepreneur to be in control of your business destiny? Can you find that in a job? Leandra Medine made the decision to become an entrepreneur, yet she realizes that is not the only way to go to feel empowered:

People ask what advice I would give to a young woman interested in becoming an entrepreneur. My answer is, if you can feel fulfilled and happy working for someone else, do that. Being a woman in power does not mean a woman who runs her own business. You can be an incredibly empowered woman within the context of another's organization. And guess what? Your boss could also be male and white, and you could still be the most powerful version of yourself.

I asked Leandra if she had it to do over again, would she take a job in media to learn more before starting her own company? Does she recommend gaining a greater body of knowledge before making that entrepreneurial move?

> I say to women who are in their formative years, who are trying to figure out what they want to do with their lives and where they want to go, because so much of the messaging is such that in order to succeed, you have to be a "girl boss," I'm not sure if that's necessarily true. It would have been really hard for me to work long term for someone else because I've always had this idea that I should be the government of a country.
>
> I don't mean that literally. I just mean that I always wanted to do things differently, and I never understood why that would not be possible. But not everyone thinks that way, and it is okay if you don't. As a matter of fact, it's really valuable if you don't think that way. You can make your value known, iterate, and explore that value in other capacities, in ways that don't leave you dry heaving because people management is so challenging.

A lot of people think that starting their own business is like a rocket ship to stardom, celebrity, and money, especially with a high-profile company like Man Repeller that took off so quickly. One of the biggest challenges in business is growing it and managing the people, along with all the pressures of running it. Good people management is a skill. I asked Leandra if she found that a challenge in her growing company and if being an entrepreneur brought out aspects of her personality she wasn't otherwise aware of.

> It requires you to confront a lot of your demons that you don't want to know. It forces you to confront these things that are really challenging for you, that you may never have had to experience or recognize as qualities you maintain if you were not in the position that you are.

I always thought that I was such a people person. But I am not detail oriented, and in that lack of detail orientation sits a lot of what makes being a good manager of an organization or a good manager of people within an organization. So when I am tasked with the role of managing, I find myself having to question these former versions of what I have assumed as facts about myself. Then I'm thinking, "Well, this is not true. What else in that is true about me?" That's really scary. That's been really hard for me. It's also the most important part of the business. I'm convinced that you could have the worst idea ever, but if you have a really smart and competent team, you will succeed.

One of my goals in the class I teach is to break down the walls between different kinds of businesses because the same general principles apply. If that were truly understood, creativity could flourish. Different points of view are valuable when developing any kind of product or service. Dennis Crowley shared the things he has in common with other business leaders:

> I meet lots of leaders from all sorts of different companies all the time, and we all have exactly the same problems, which are growing the company, retaining key talent, fighting off copycats, all the operations stuff is always a pain in the ass, finance, HR and making sure everyone is happy, and management and training managers. This stuff spreads across all of these businesses.
>
> When you look at what's happening today, this month, this quarter, it's all, "Man, where the hell is this thing going?" Every company goes through the same thing. Just no one ever talks about it.
>
> I'm going to tell you what's going to happen before you even launch. It's going to go up, and then it's going to get flat, and then what are you going to do? You've got to have a plan for what happens after it gets flat because it always gets flat. You've got to figure out, what do you do? How are you different?

How do you stand out? How do you keep people motivated? How do you keep them compensated? That's where the challenge from all of this stuff ends up, but that's not sexy to talk about, so no one talks about it.

Some of the shittiest times in my career, my life, were after the Dodgeball stuff was gone. I didn't have an audience. I didn't have a project. I didn't have a database. I didn't have a platform. I had this mental block of "I already tried that. I can't do that thing again. You can't start another band and sing the same songs. You've got to do something else." I just couldn't find anything else I wanted to do. I was telling the story about Google shutting it down, which was the cathartic moment of "Okay, now it doesn't exist. Now I can build it again."

Most of us put things off because we're afraid to take the leap into the unknown. When I was considering moving from Madison, Wisconsin, where I went to college, to New York City, I got more questions than support. "Do you have a job lined up?" "Do you know where you're going to live?" "Do you know people there?" "Aren't you afraid of what might happen if you move there?" I was more afraid of what would happen if I stayed. Fortunately, my parents were completely supportive. I was young, ambitious, unattached—the perfect time to make a move. Why not? I moved to New York. I had things I wanted to do, but no goals. It was about the journey, not the destination.

It's interesting to see if there is a gap between what we thought we wanted and what we've become, whether we are happy about the decisions we've made and what we've learned. In so many cases, what we loved doing when we were kids and why we stopped doing it created two lanes. One lane was what you love doing, and the other is what you think you should be doing. For most people, as time passes, the space between the two lanes gets farther apart. So many of us have feelings we are afraid to share because of a fear of criticism, which is why so many of our lives split into those two lanes in the first place.

Workbook Questions

- 💡 Why do you want to do what you are pursuing? What motivates you?

- 💡 What ways could you develop multiple income streams from what you do? Write them down.

- 💡 What are the character traits of a person you would want to work for? How does your personality compare to that?

- 💡 How do you react when you confront an obstacle?

- 💡 How do you deal with stress?

- 💡 Knowing what you know now, what advice would you give your younger self?

- 💡 How, on a personal level, do you define success?

CONCLUSION

Advice to Your Younger Self

THE LAST QUESTION I ASK my guests is, "Knowing what you know now, what advice would you give your younger self as you were starting out?"

> I had this yearning that started as a whisper, "This is not you." It became a very loud scream because I wasn't listening to the voice of how out-of-touch I felt. I don't know who I am or why I'm here or what my gifts are to give, but I'm going on a quest to answer those questions. That's what led me to begin making art, writing more publicly and following the path of wonder that I went on.
>
> My younger self was so caught up in how other people perceived me that I would tell my younger self, "No one's actually thinking about you anyway. They're thinking about themselves—so go do whatever damn thing you want to do."
>
> **—AMBER RAE**

> Drink more water and learn to be okay with hearing no. Not everybody's going to love everything that you do, and that's okay.
>
> **—OLIVER JEFFERS**

I wish I could go back and tell young Randi that the things about me that were unique would be the things that would ultimately make me succeed in business. It wasn't until I stopped suppressing those things inside of me that I actually started inventing things that were great, that I started having ideas that were great, that I did things I was proud of. So don't shelve the things that make you you for people who are never going to be pleased by you anyway.

—RANDI ZUCKERBERG

It's not nearly as important as it seems in the moment, so don't worry about it.

—LAURA EDWARDS

Be fearless. I know it sounds so cliché, but you have to be fearless in whatever you approach. You have to evaluate: What's the downside? I might get a no, but I'm going to be in no different a place than had I not done it at all. So why not try it? Don't listen to naysayers. Don't listen to the outside noise. Keep focused.

—STEPHANIE JONES

Don't be afraid to speak up if you're uncomfortable in situations because I feel like there's so many instances that I would go and cry and think to myself, "What should I do?" I wouldn't call any one. I wouldn't leave. I wouldn't say anything. Nothing's going to get done and nothing's going to change because I haven't done anything to change it. I would definitely tell my younger self, speak up and don't be afraid of making people feel uncomfortable because they've already made you feel uncomfortable. Say something.

—LEOMIE ANDERSON

Ask for help. Don't think that you can figure out this whole life thing by yourself. To falsely believe that you and you alone can be successful or have a great career or find love, whatever the thing is, you're just not that good. Nobody is. We're social animals for a reason because we take care of each other and we need each other. When we're willing to ask for help and accept it when it's offered, it is not a sign of weakness. It is a sign of absolute strength. I wish I asked for more help and admitted that I didn't know things when I was younger.

—SIMON SINEK

While it is important to have career goals, life tends to happen nonlinearly, and quite frankly, most successful people have also enjoyed strokes of luck. Instead of focusing on a long-range plan, focus on what is in your control today and be the best at the job in front of you. Use that as a springboard into the next thing. Then, as Steve Jobs said, connect the dots looking backward.

—DANIEL GULATI

Focus. Work hard. Be a nice person, and everything's going to be okay in the end.

—YUKO SHIMIZU

You'll get from A to B with a lot of squiggles in between. A career path and life path is nonlinear; it's a winding road. If you are never satisfied with success, if you are never complacent with failure, you will get toys.

—SARAH MASLIN NIR

I would tell my younger self to make the demand that, in pursuit of your goals, you should love what you do and be passionate about it. I sold eight and a half years of my life very cheaply because I was chasing money. If I had just made the demand that you can make a lot of money doing something that you believe in, and that you're passionate about, and I didn't.

    —TOM BILYEU

Get out of Alabama! Leave! Why are you still here doing prank calls for ten years? They're never going to hire you; they're never going to give you health care. You're working at Golden Corral and sleeping in a Ford Focus in strange truck stops. You can do that in Los Angeles for much cheaper.

    —ROY WOOD JR.

Chill out. I've spent so much of my life in a stressful tizzy, all the time thinking that's all going to go up in the air. I just think different things mattered to me three years ago that matter to me now. I needed validation. I needed love and people to like me. I needed all of that attention. Once I had a taste of that, I realized how it doesn't make you feel any different at all. I would have just told myself that this is not what matters. That's the one thing I've taken away from my life and my career in general is that this is a slippery slope. We all want to be loved and accepted and for people to like us. You have to just keep riding through.

    —BRANDON MAXWELL

WHEN I WAS much younger and embarking on my professional journey, I wanted to gain the knowledge of how to lead a fulfilling life. A life that was sustainable, emotionally and intellectually satisfying, coupled with making enough money that I could do what I wanted to, when I wanted to, and say no to all the things I didn't want to deal with.

I heard about a legendary life coach who lived deep in the Mojave Desert. Many people believed he had the secret to living a long, sustainable life. I wanted to meet him. It cost a lot. It was complicated and hard to get to him, but if I could gain that knowledge, it would be worth it. It was a long, arduous hike, but I finally made it to my destination.

He had a beatific face. Calm. Unlined by age, with a cherubic smile. He offered me mint tea. The taste and aroma could not have been better. We sat on the floor by the fire.

"You are a seeker," he said to me in a calm, almost monotone, yet soothing voice. "You are trying to find the secret."

I nodded, mesmerized by the whole setting.

"Everyone who comes here is seeking the answer." He took a sip of tea and closed his eyes, motioning to me to do the same. It was as if channeling a force from another place.

"Do you feel what I am feeling?"

I had no idea what he was feeling, but I nodded my head.

"I feel that you have questions, important questions, you want me to answer. Nod your head if you agree." I nodded, wondering how he could tell, if his eyes were still closed.

"You see darkness, but not blackness. You see the reddish warm glow from the light of the fire. Is that right?"

I nodded.

"Turn your left palm to the floor."

I did.

"Take three, slow, deep breaths."

I did.

"Extend your arm until your palm feels the power of the flame. It will hurt at first, but trust me, you will learn how to turn off the pain and embrace the warmth."

"Are you crazy?" I opened my eyes. "I'm not going to stick my hand in the fire."

"Good. You're not a total idiot. Want a beer?"

He popped the caps off with a jeweled bottle opener. "Real diamonds. It was a gift. Gotta be a fool to spend that kind of money on a bottle opener." He handed me a beer.

"You had a lot invested in hiking through the desert to find me. You think somebody's got the answer for your burning, pardon the pun, questions? If anyone does, it's you—not me. I don't even know you." He laughed. "You wouldn't believe all the goofs that stick their hand in the fire. I always knock their hand away before they burn it. This is the middle of nowhere. You hurt yourself, you are fucked big time."

I told him I heard he had the secret to what seemed like eternal life.

"You live here, dealing with people who think I have all the answers, it seems like eternity." He took a long sip of beer. "You had the persistence to set up the meeting, the commitment to come here, and the perseverance and stamina to make the hike. Now all you need to do is apply that to your career because I can't do shit for you." He took another long sip.

I asked him why he did it.

"It's a living."

The moral of the story is, you have to do the work. There is no magic portal to pass through. There is no secret. Part of making a living with your ideas involves maintaining sustainable energy by taking care of yourself, having unbounded curiosity and the desire for discovery, so you are inspired to keep coming up with ideas. It also requires being able to create a long-term sustainable business, which means exercising sound business principles and being aware of the risks that are involved. Making a living with your ideas is a marathon, not a sprint. There will be rewards, emotionally, intellectually, and financially, but they are the by-product of the work you do.

THANK YOU

I'M GRATEFUL TO A LOT of people who helped me on the path of teaching and learning, which led to writing this book:

My wife, Margaret, and children, Audrey and Jake, who keep me grounded, put up with me, and constantly help and surprise me—usually in a good way.

My parents, Lily and Ralph Madoff, who encouraged me to be curious and do whatever I wanted to do as long as I found it fulfilling and treated people well.

My lifelong friends Ken Mirman, Ellis Berns, Doug Fielding, Ralph Capriolo, and Rebecca Adamson. We laugh together, call each other's bullshit, and are there at 3:00 a.m. when the going gets tough.

My fourth-grade teacher, Mrs. Ripley, who showed me how a great teacher teaches.

Dean Stadel, who introduced me to Parsons as a guest lecturer and encouraged me to teach.

The students at Parsons who made every semester a joy—not all of you, but most of you.

The many guests in my Creative Careers class who share their insights with us, are so generous with their time, and introduce me to other great guests. I wish I could have included all of you, but if this sells, there will be a sequel, so there is still a chance.

Jodi Lipper, the wonderful writer, for her generosity of spirit. Jodi introduced me to her agent because she believed in the book. She also wrote the excellent proposal that got the book sold.

Brandi Bowles, who so effectively and enthusiastically represented the book and didn't care that I didn't have a large social media following—she actually believed in the value of the book.

Dan Ambrosio, senior editor at Hachette Go, who liked, supported, and bought the book—otherwise you wouldn't be reading this now.

Lauren Marino, who helped me structure the book and kept me organized—not easy.

My executive producer, Ed Daly, for his dedication and integrity in running my business so I can do the other things I do.

INDEX